THE
WOODPECKER'S
PURPOSE

WALTER R. THORSON

THE WOODPECKER'S PURPOSE

A CRITIQUE OF INTELLIGENT DESIGN

WALTER R. THORSON

Made possible by a grant from the
JOHN TEMPLETON FOUNDATION
in partnership with the Center for Faith and Inquiry at Gordon College

Emily Ruppel, Editor

**CENTER FOR
FAITH AND INQUIRY**
AT GORDON COLLEGE

Center for Faith and Inquiry at Gordon College
255 Grapevine Road, Wenham, MA 01984
cfi@gordon.edu
978.867.4227

Printed in the United States of America

ISBN-13:978-0692220337
ISBN-10:069222033X

Library of Congress data on file

Designed and typeset by Rusty and Ingrid Creative Company
www.rustyandingrid.com

Cover Illustration by Louis Agassiz Fuertes of a Red-headed Woodpecker (Melanerpes erythrocephalus). Source: http://commons.wikimedia.org/wiki/File:Redhead_the_Woodpecker,_Downy_the_Woodpecker.jpg

To my wife, Mary Elizabeth:

For minutes logged waiting for me at mealtimes;

For hours spent alone while I thought about and wrote this work;

For years listening to me talk about this and other academic pursuits;

And for being my lifelong "heir together of the grace of life."

TABLE OF CONTENTS

FOREWORD

This book by Walter Thorson represents the first in a new series, The Herrmann Lectures at Gordon College, sponsored by The John Templeton Foundation. I was honored to be given this named lectureship by virtue of my long association with Sir John Templeton, a man of remarkable vision and foresight who first dazzled the investment world by his business skill and then turned his attention to his first love, examining the way new scientific discoveries open up fascinating theological questions. John's insatiable curiosity and inventive genius became evident at an early age, and was given ample opportunity to develop in several directions through wise and very encouraging parents. After graduation from his high school in Winchester, Tennessee, John was accepted at Yale University, the only student from his high school ever to be so honored, and was subsequently selected for Phi Beta Kappa and enrolled at Oxford's Baliol College, as a Rhodes Scholar. In 1987 he established The John Templeton Foundation, devoted to the study of a new discipline, the interaction of science and religion.

The author of the present book is no stranger to this new discipline. Walter Thorson was educated in California and Boston, receiving his doctorate from The California Institute of Technology and post doctorate training from Harvard University. He subsequently joined the faculty at M.I.T. in Theoretical Chemistry where he did research and teaching until moving to the University of Alberta in 1968. Early in his career he had developed a keen interest in biblical and philosophical aspects of scientific truth which involved a lively interchange with other American Scientific Affiliation members, mostly through the pages of *Perspectives in Science and Christian Faith* (PSCF). After moving to Alberta he also accepted an appointment as Adjunct Professor of the Philosophy of Science at Regent College, Vancouver, B. C. and taught courses in epistemology of religious knowledge, philosophy of science, and later on, scientific and biblical accounts of origins.

Thorson's book, *The Woodpecker's Purpose: A Critique of Intelligent Design*, represents his thoughts, carefully weighed and measured, after much discussion with respondents and others involved in the lecture series. Professor Thorson has given us a scholarly examination of the intelligent design argument along with a fresh view of biology as having some surprising elements which carry beyond the usual mechanistic approach to evolution, bringing in teleological aspects often shunned by the scientific community. He nevertheless stoutly defends the theological legitimacy of naturalism as a presupposition in science.

What is different about biology, he says, is its level of organization, which is arranged with a view to specific function. He says there is an essential continuity in the gradual development of some degree of purposeful behavior in living things. And the presence of organization toward function is an essential element in that progression. Thinking about biology in new ways that are not purely mechanistic or causal suggests that a "limited kind of teleology" is relevant in this case. He notes that there is a risk here, but we should be guided by what is <u>real</u>.

This approach, he says, offers an opportunity for Christians to speak out, doing good science but searching for ways to examine this very important possibility more fully. Walter is an evangelical Christian, who has shared his faith unabashedly throughout his long career, beginning in academia in California and then in Boston and New England primarily with Intervarsity Christian Fellowship and then overseas at places like Schloss Mittersil In Europe. His forthright examination of his faith, especially as it relates to questions of philosophy and to biblical understanding are refreshing and challenging. Certainly, this book deserves careful reading.

—Robert L. Herrmann

CHAPTER 1:

INTRODUCTION

I and my coauthors in this work are "academics" by background; that is, we are either currently active as university teachers, or (as in my case) are retired from that profession. Many of us are scientifically trained, and have a good understanding of the principles and practice of scientific research; a few had careers in physical science or related disciplines in mathematics and information theory, while others are biologists. Still others are associated with academic life as professors and teachers in areas such as Christian theology and biblical scholarship.

Further, we are Christians; that is, we believe the teachings of the Christian religion and are seriously committed as persons to the personal God who speaks in both Old and New Testaments. Some have considerable experience in the Christian communities formed in churches and other Christian organizations. That experience flavors our approach to issues such as "intelligent design." We are not academic outsiders looking into the subject as merely an interesting cultural phenomenon; it matters to us if our fellow Christians believe the claims of intelligent design advocates. It also matters to us what friends think who are *not* Christians. If people suppose that intelligent design represents what thinking Christians really believe about creation, there is a problem for Christian apologetics. Hence one of our aims is a corrective to such misunderstanding—an "apology" in both senses of that word.

Thirdly, as Christians we all affirm that God is indeed the "creator of heaven and earth—of all things, visible and invisible." We use the terms *cosmos* or *cosmology* in their proper and limited scientific context, but for us they have no deep religious or philosophical meaning. The assertion that God created all things is an essential element of both Judaism and Christianity; philosophically, it assures human beings that nothing is beyond his power, his justice—or his mercy, if it is sought by them. This understanding of God is central to Old Testament thought, and has a very practical meaning, illustrated nicely in Psalm 96:5: "The gods of the nations are (only) idols; but the LORD made the heavens."[1] The New Testament repeats the practical point of the argument: For example, St. Paul at Athens: "The God who made the world and everything in it, being Lord of heaven and earth, does not live in shrines made by men... since he himself gives to all persons their life and breath and everything" (Acts 17:24).

Finally, because scientific questions are involved in issues discussed here, it is important that such discussion be scientifically competent and also be done with integrity in relation to the truth. To the best of our ability, I and my coauthors are committed to these aims.

NATURAL SCIENCE AND / OR NATURAL THEOLOGY?

It is necessary to make a distinction first between these two very different kinds of thinking about the natural world. Of the two, natural theology is older by far; while the ancient world gave some rudimentary attention to problems in natural science, these were often inseparable from philosophical or religious ideas pervading ancient culture. Natural *science* as we understand it today is quite recent, dating back only about four or five centuries.

Since the medieval period in Western culture, natural *theology* has been a discourse about the world carried on in the context of the belief that the entire world is the creation of God—in particular, the biblical God confessed by both Jews and Christians. Of these two faiths, Christianity has the more highly public tradition of philosophical reflection, dating back to Medieval and scholastic roots in the twelfth century or earlier; Judaism's traditions of thought about creation are rich but less well known, though the whole world has benefited from important Jewish insights about creation from the Rabbinic tradition over nearly two thousand years.

As its name suggests, natural theology is mainly concerned with the relations between God and his creation. It asks questions about (a) what we can learn about God from the character of creation, or (b) what we might think about the creation and its properties, based on what we believe about God. It is particularly motivated by assertions made in both Old and New Testaments that creation exhibits or displays God's glory, wisdom and power. Such assertions are in no way weakened by the increased understanding of the world and its order we have learned from scientific inquiry; it just isn't the case that scientific knowledge removes our sense of wonder at the world's complexity and variety.

I (and many of my coauthors) think that arguments for (or *against*) intelligent design *are* appropriate—provided they are understood as arguments in natural theology; indeed, this book is such a discussion. However, we do *not* believe these arguments have any place or legitimacy in the quite separate discourse called natural *science*.

Natural *science* (in contrast to natural theology) is a discourse about the character and order of the world, conducted *without* making any assertions or statements about it as God's creation. In fact, since the rise of modern science in the later 1600's it has been understood that such assertions or claims are not legitimate *scientific* explanations of natural things and natural phenomena, even though scientists themselves may personally believe in God as the creator. Natural science is conducted according to the rule that explaining things and events in the world must be done without implicating God as an agent or cause. This rule is not arbitrary; the basis for it is soundly based in reason and experience, a point I shall argue more fully in Chapter 3.

Most issues in contemporary debate about intelligent design arise from the failure to understand, or the refusal to acknowledge, that there should exist any such distinction between natural theology and natural science.

As a rule, people who argue for intelligent design reject the distinction, while practicing scientists either accept it—or have no room for natural theology in their thinking about the world.

PHILOSOPHICAL NATURALISM AND / OR METHODOLOGICAL NATURALISM

A parallel distinction is needed between philosophical naturalism and methodological naturalism, terms defined briefly as follows:

As its name suggests, *philosophical naturalism* (sometimes also called *metaphysical* naturalism) is a world-view to which God is unnecessary. When physicist and mathematician Simon LaPlace was asked by the French emperor Napoleon whether his nebular hypothesis for the formation of the solar system required him to assume divine agency as a force, he famously replied: "Sire, I found no need of that hypothesis." In today's world, much the same attitude permeates all cultural thinking, and many people conduct their lives and daily affairs on the assumption that real events and their consequences are to be decided without reference to God's agency.

In Psalm 1, a blessing is given to the person "who does not walk in the counsel of the ungodly." People mistakenly assume that the "counsel of the ungodly" is advice to act immorally or dishonestly; the Psalmist is really speaking of a general *attitude* that leaves God out of life's choices. A person who lives in awe of God cannot be a *philosophical* naturalist.

In strong contrast to this is the concept of *methodological naturalism*. As its name suggests, it is a presupposition adopted for the purpose of certain *limited* kinds (or methods) of inquiry or study. In particular, it is a fundamental presupposition of natural science, one that all working scientists understand. I have used Simon LaPlace's famous remark intentionally in the preceding passage, because I think both LaPlace and Napoleon were men who really saw the modern world as one in which God is irrelevant to *all* thinking and action. But as a *scientist*, I actually agree with LaPlace's view of planetary formation as a hypothesis into which we should *not* introduce God's agency. Like all scientists, I argue that scientific enquiry should not invoke divine agency as an explanation of those things and phenomena open to it.

However, we all recognize that there must be *some* point in "scientific" discourse where the methodological adoption of naturalism may limit our ability to understand reality. For example, most thoughtful people recognize that *behaviorist psychology* does not offer adequate understanding of human personality. Is psychology a *science* in the same sense physics is?

Present debate over intelligent design arises because its proponents argue that methodological naturalism is inadequate even for *biology*.

A BRIEF SUMMARY OF CHAPTERS 2–7

Chapter 2 is a reflection on four Psalms that look at creation in this context. I believe that a better sense of the biblical perspective on creation as God's "*handiwork*" will help us appreciate more fully the theological and philosophical issues at stake in current debate about "intelligent design."

Chapter 3 looks in some detail at the underlying historical and philosophical reasons why the scientific tradition is "naturalistic." How we think about that naturalistic tradition affects our understanding of scientific questions.

Chapter 4 is a commentary on contemporary culture. No adequate discussion of important issues (such as intelligent design) can ignore its emerging problems and failures. To the extent that Christian subculture partakes in these, its particular concerns will be marked by these same problems and weaknesses, especially North American evangelical Christian subculture.

Chapter 5 gives a brief history of the modern intelligent design movement since ~1980.[2] Contrary to much secular opinion, contemporary proponents of intelligent design are not uneducated or ignorant persons. Some have advanced degrees in science, philosophy, or theology, and in addition have taken the trouble to further educate themselves on particular topics in biological science they deem relevant to their arguments and conclusions. Some of us are acquainted personally with these writers and respect their reasoning ability and intelligence, even though we disagree radically with their conclusions about biology. I have attempted to be as neutral as possible in this history of "ID."

Chapter 6 turns to the scientific issues at stake in the discussion. Because such questions never have exhaustive and final answers, we all understand that our claims as to what is true are always *tentative*, open to change as better understanding of the world emerges. I have included in my discussion a number of items I considered relevant in some fashion to the debate. As a physical scientist not intimately acquainted with technical issues in biology, my own arguments are not unflawed, and important contributions by others address these issues more competently. All of us remain open to further dialogue with people who ask thoughtful questions within the context of this work.

I conclude my contribution to this work with Chapter 7, which discusses philosophical questions. In particular, I challenge the capacity of radical evolutionary arguments (often called "Deep Darwinism") to "explain" or "complete" our understanding of the world, or of ourselves as intelligent agents within it.

INTELLIGENT DESIGN ARGUMENTS FOCUS ON BIOLOGY

While some proponents of intelligent design claim that *in principle* their philosophical arguments apply equally to the modern sciences of cosmology, geology, astronomy, and related studies of *physical* origins, most of them focus on an argument for design in biology. They argue that the complexity and specific organization of living things cannot be explained as the result of evolutionary change (*e.g.*, as described by the neo-Darwinian hypothesis).

An important issue, therefore, is whether or not the methods found effective in the physical sciences (physics, chemistry and their applications to geology, astronomy, and other topics where living things are not the object of study) are also appropriate for the study of living things. Authors of this book argue for methodological naturalism in biology.

ID proponents often reply to this line of argument by claiming that "*biology* is different" from the physical sciences. I happen to agree with them on this specific point, but the detailed nature of this difference is a topic of some discussion here. While I and my coauthors argue about that, we all agree it does not require ID to explain it.

THEOLOGICAL AND PHILOSOPHICAL PERSPECTIVE

I make frequent reference in this work to the philosophical ideas of the Hungarian scientist, sociologist and philosopher Michael Polanyi. Most of Polanyi's important ideas are about knowing as a *dynamic process*: How scientific discovery actually happens, and what it means to know something—whether the knowledge is inarticulate and tacit (like recognizing a face in a crowd as a person we know), or partly articulate and formal (as in language, mathematics and the sciences). Polanyi's insights have shaped much of my understanding about philosophical issues, but understanding him takes effort. I include below a citation to the one work by Polanyi I think indispensable to mastering his ideas.[3]

CHAPTER 2:

FOUR CREATION PSALMS

INTRODUCTION

I sometimes find that when I defend the tradition of methodological naturalism in science to communities with Christian belief, I am seen as somehow sharing a lack of awe for creation as God's handiwork, or as taking for granted the incredible beauty and complexity of what our Lord has made. This is far from the case. Throughout my working life as a professional scientist and still today I have given a good deal of thought to the question: *How do the human authors of scripture think about creation and its relation to God?* In this chapter I try to suggest an answer to that question.

Since New Testament writers think and write within the milieu of their understanding of the Old Testament, their remarks about creation are informed by its pattern of thought. Learning to read and understand the Old Testament as Scripture for its own sake (rather than using it merely as a basis for New Testament interpretations or glosses) has been a revitalizing part of my life, both as a scholar and as a Christian seeking to know God personally, like many people in the Old Testament.

I believe this chapter's reflections on four "creation Psalms"—reflections in *natural theology*, if you like—will help define the context in which I make arguments criticizing intelligent design as an approach to the *natural science* of biology. I do not consider these four to be an exhaustive collection, but they show a clear progression of thought about creation and God.

PSALM 19

The heavens are telling the glory of God; and the firmament proclaims his handiwork. Day to day pours forth speech, and night to night declares knowledge. There is no speech, nor are there words; their voice is not heard; yet their voice goes out through all the earth, and their words to the end of the world.

In them he has set a tent for the sun, which comes forth like a bridegroom leaving his chamber, and like a strong man, runs its course with joy. Its rising is from the end of the heavens, and its circuit to the end of them; and there is nothing hid from its heat.

The law of the LORD is perfect, reviving the soul; the testimony of the LORD is sure, making wise the simple; the precepts of the LORD are right, rejoicing the heart; the commandment of the LORD is pure, enlightening the eyes; the fear of the LORD is clean, enduring forever; the ordinances of the LORD are true, and righteous altogether. More to be desired are they than gold, even much fine gold; sweeter also than honey and the drippings of the honeycomb. Moreover, by them is thy servant warned; in keeping them there is great reward.

But who can discern his errors? Clear thou me from hidden faults. Keep back thy servant also from presumptuous sins; let them not have dominion over me! Then I shall be blameless, and innocent of great transgression. Let the words of my mouth and the meditation of my heart be acceptable in thy sight, O LORD, my rock and my redeemer.

It has been said that each of the three great cultures influencing Western civilization, Greek, Roman and Hebrew, placed special emphasis on a physical sense of perception that represented a primary focus of attention for that culture. Each has left its mark on our abstract language for knowledge or understanding. For example, when we say "I see the point you're making," or "I can't quite grasp the idea," we reflect the influence of Greek and Roman conceptions of knowledge, respectively.

For Greeks, the central epistemic or *knowing* experience is the moment of *integration*, when subsidiary particulars come together, forming a complete and meaningful picture for us[1]. The experience is universal to human beings, and we all vividly remember such moments of insight in our lives. But Greek culture especially emphasizes it. Perhaps it is best epitomized by Greek philosophy, striving to give an overall picture of the world by which we can govern our lives and give them meaning. But Greek poetry and art have the same emphasis: Homer's *Odyssey* speaks of *grey-eyed* Athena, who sprang full grown from the mind or forehead of Zeus, guides Odysseus on his journey home from Troy and is the source of his understanding at crucial points. Other visual images such as "the wine-dark sea" or "dawn, the rosy-fingered" convey images of reality we ourselves retain from life-long experience. Classical Greek sculpture amazes us by its capacity to capture in stone some things our own eyes also have seen. Like the Greeks, we moderns also tend to make the moment of integration, the moment when we finally "get the picture" or "see it all," as the focal point in abstract, conceptual understanding.

For Roman culture, the statement "knowledge is power" summarizes a different stage in knowing: That stage following the experience of integration, when something we have understood is assimilated as a tool we use confidently to shape the world. That's exemplified in the major concrete achievements by which we remember the Roman Empire: law, architecture, roads, armies, and governmental authority. Correspondingly, a major preoccupation for many Roman authors and historians was to maintain permanence of an ordered human society.[2]

Psalm 19 presents the very different approach to knowledge we have received from Hebrew culture: a focus on its *source*. The Old Testament prophets are often extraordinarily visual in their language (Isaiah speaks constantly of vision, often unshared with others; Ezekiel tells us how God continually asked him "Son of man, do you see this?"). However, the underlying source of enlightenment for the Hebrews is unmistakable: "The word of the LORD came to me, saying …"

The heavens on a starry night are surely the most overwhelming visual experience we can have; yet the Hebrew poet uses an *auditory* metaphor to describe it, saying that they are telling us about the glory of God, and that they tell all human beings everywhere of his creative power and wisdom. What understanding lies behind this attitude toward knowing?

Hearing, like seeing and grasping, provides an epistemic metaphor. It describes the stage *before* the "visual" point of integration, when we are most dependent on what is *other than ourselves* to provide clues for us to make sense of. It is therefore also the least egocentric stage, and it emphasizes in our experience the belief that what is being perceived is objective, that is, *other* than ourselves. Finally, it also emphasizes the incompleteness of our knowledge.

Yet, if we take the element of our personal involvement in knowing as the key to a sound epistemology, as Michael Polanyi does, this is the exciting and pivotal moment in discovery—the point at which we first recognize that a collection of particulars that has somehow attracted our attention *may* have a greater meaning as a whole.

Years ago, our family was camping in the Canadian Rockies in early fall, and my five-year old son and I needed to answer a call of nature on a bitterly cold and clear night. As we both stood there shivering and wanting most to go back to the tent and get warm again, he looked up at the splendor above and said: "*WOW!!*" In that one word he explained Psalm 19's language.

The truth is that when we look at the heavens, we do not understand (in the Greek or Roman senses) the glory of God, or the nature and depth of his craftsmanship and creative power; instead, we are beggared by the experience, and only the most incorrigibly self-centered of human beings can regard the spectacle as mundane or a matter of course. Several young astronomers were college acquaintances, and it always impressed me that their sense of awe at the universe we were learning about scientifically was in each case as genuine as my own. I'm glad one or two of them have since become confessing Christians; it confirms the divine authenticity in our youthful sense of awe at the creation's witness to its maker.

Of course, the Hebrew author of Psalm 19 was familiar with surrounding pagan societies, so we can also "read between the lines" of his poem. He understands that Genesis 1's account of the creation of sun, moon and stars on the fourth day is an implicit polemic about worshipping the heavens. The sun and moon are only prescribed regulators over the days and seasons for the sake of the *living* creation (*Don't worship them—they're only bureaucrats!*), and the "vast array" astronomers now recognize as being each a sun in its own right is dismissed as subsidiary to these two ("he made the stars also"). Moderns may focus on the scientific naivety of the poet, or *instead* begin to think after him.

After he describes the heavens as declaring rather than fully manifesting God's glory, the poet moves on to speak of the sun. His language is restrained; obviously he doesn't worship the sun, but sees it as something to be enjoyed, just as the sheep and the forest and the meadows are. Yet there's a point in his language: The sun makes its daily circuit, bringing warmth and life to all the creation, and—a key phrase—"there is nothing hid from its heat." Majestic as the stars are, they don't do that for people. And now comes the real point of the poem: the analogy in its second stanza.

Christians love to recite the couplets in Psalm 19 about the law and teachings of the LORD. One benefit of modern church songs is the way they teach us Hebrew poetry, a rhyming more of related ideas than of words. Here the Psalmist is pointing out the bright stars in God's moral firmament, and you can enjoy the pleasure of savoring his recital for yourself. At the end, the third-person description of God's law turns to a direct address in prayer to God himself: "Moreover, by them your servant is warned; in keeping them there is great reward."

This captures what sincere rabbinic Judaism has striven to emphasize as faithfulness to God: appreciating, revering, and meditating on Torah, and obeying its teachings from the heart. Messiah did not say he had come to set aside the Law, but rather to fulfill it. Christians must not see the gospel as something that ignores Torah; true Christianity isn't manifest in the careless moral lives and shallow talk of much evangelical profession in America these days.

But having directed his attention to God himself, the poet now speaks to the LORD as being the sun of his spiritual life. "There is nothing hid from its heat" is now fully developed into a prayer to a God who knows us each fully: Lord, keep me from the mold and rot of presumptuous, arrogant evildoing; keep me from developing fungal growths that don't belong in the sunshine of your presence. And not only my daily habits and actions; LORD, let my words, which lead me to actions, and the inner thoughts of my heart, manifest in my words and actions, be acceptable in your sight. Any true servant of God will affirm this prayer!

Like most psalms, Psalm 19 takes our thinking from desperate need or an appreciative mood toward a personal address in prayer to God himself. However, it also begins a reflective process that moves on to other psalms for fuller development. The four "creation psalms" discussed in this essay are neither a complete set, nor exclusive of other fruitful sequences for reflection on the Psalms. But I have enjoyed this set as one showing where reflection on creation can take us. Psalm 19 begins with the heavens and their declaration of God's glory, and ends with prayer for deeper personal openness to God as creator and redeemer. Let us go on to the second Psalm in the sequence.

PSALM 8

O LORD, our Lord, how majestic is thy name in all the earth!

Thou whose glory above the heavens is chanted by the mouth of babes and infants: thou hast founded a bulwark because of thy foes, to still the enemy and the avenger

When I look at the heavens, the work of thy fingers, the moon and stars which thou hast established: what is man that thou are mindful of him, and the son of man that thou dost care for him?

Yet thou hast made him little less than God, and dost crown him with glory and honor. Thou hast given him dominion over the works of thy hands; thou hast put all things under his feet: all sheep and oxen, and also the beasts of the field, the birds of the air, and the fish of the sea, whatever passes along the paths of the sea.

O LORD, our Lord, how majestic is thy name in all the earth!

This psalm has been given a rich exposition in the New Testament's Letter to the Hebrews.[3] While we're concerned here with its Old Testament context, it is helpful to summarize what the author of Hebrews says concerning the true humanity of Messiah. Hebrews 2:4-6 cites part of Psalm 8 as follows:

"What is man that thou are mindful of him, or the son of man, that thou carest for him? Thou didst make him for a little while lower than the angels; thou hast crowned him with glory and honor, putting everything in subjection under his feet."

The significant variation here is the change from "little less than God" to "for a little while lower than the angels." I'm not qualified to comment on its textual legitimacy, but it is pertinent to the author's argument.

The psalm celebrates the condition of humanity in its idyllic unfallen state, as described in Genesis 2. There's no hint of the succeeding events, except in the preceding verses referring to an enemy to be silenced. But the author of Hebrews argues that the Psalm as it stands cannot really be *true*: We do not see all things subject to "man"—and here the author is not speaking specifically of Messiah, but of humanity generically—just as David does in the psalm. The evidence for that is our being subject to death, a point elaborated by the author in his exposition. Emily Dickinson's poem "Because I could not stop for death, he kindly stopped for me"[4] says it very well. But the author of Hebrews argues that the psalm *is* fulfilled in prospect through the humanity, suffering and resurrection of Jesus the Messiah, who takes up all of humanity into his own flesh and blood and represents them toward God, the main theme of the rest of his letter.

There is also a mystical element in the psalm, implicit in the Hebrews 2 discussion, and evident in Matthew's account of Jesus in the temple after the triumphal entry (Matthew 21:12-17). Jesus quotes a variant of verse 1b-2a: "out of the mouths of babes and infants you have brought perfect praise." By doing this he says to those rejecting his claim to be Messiah: Yes, I hear them, and it *is* appropriate, because I have come to fulfill Messiah's work. The mystical insight lies in the phrase immediately following (verse 2b: "to silence the enemy and the avenger"): Christ reminds those who are supposed to know the meaning of the psalm to think about what he has really come to do for humanity enslaved by the devil. Matthew shares with us his own devotion to the Messiah as he describes the events and words spoken in his account of the passion—*here is the true King, the promised son of David.*

Now let's consider Psalm 8 in its Old Testament context as one in a train of creation psalms.

The direction begun in Psalm 19 is resumed by the reference to the work of God's fingers in the heavens and then immediate *re-direction* to humans as the real focus of divine interest (8:3-4). The text is often misunderstood as saying that human beings have no significance in the overall scheme of the universe's size and grandeur—a thoroughly modern misconception. It is actually saying just the opposite: *When I look at the majesty of the heavens, the glorious things you've created above us, how important we humans must be to you, since you pay us so much attention!* (The author of Hebrews interprets the text in the same way.)

Psalm 8 begins: "O LORD, our Lord, how majestic is your name in all the earth!" This is repeated for emphasis at the end. In the Old Testament, and especially in the Psalms, the relation between heavens and earth is a topic of frequent reference. Consider the liturgical fragment "Be exalted, O God, above the heavens; and let thy glory be over all the earth" [Ps. 57:5, 57:11; Ps. 108:5]. The prayer Messiah taught his disciples develops this: "Your kingdom come, your will be done on earth, just as it is in heaven." Psalm 8 affirms that God's name *is* majestic in all the earth, and following this: "You whose glory above the heavens is chanted." God's transcendence with respect to the heavens, implicit in Psalm 19, is now openly stated. A favorite theme in Hebrew thought runs: *The gods of the nations are (only) idols; but the LORD made the heavens.* Malachi tells God's people in rebuke that his name is universally feared among heathen nations, while *they* take him for granted. Yet an underlying theme in all these references is just the point of "the Lord's prayer": Are God's will, and the glory of his name, as openly triumphant on earth as they are in heaven? Exploring this question leads to the teaching of Hebrews 2 as the statement of Christian hope; as the author argues, "just now there's a war going on."

But let us return to the Old Testament perspective:

Psalm 8's detailed picture of human authority in creation continues, going from domestic animals to those in the wild, then to birds of the air and the fish of the sea—repeating the prospective dominion given on the sixth day by the divine blessing (Genesis 1:26-31). Significantly, though human beings are created along with the other land creatures, their dominion extends also to skies above and waters in the seas.

Because the perspective of these essays is concerned with science and human vocation, we can't avoid asking about space, often called the "last frontier." I don't think there is any implicit biblical restriction on human exploration of space, but perhaps a degree of ambivalence is proper in the *value* we place on it. First, we know that space is an alien environment for us, and that enormous risks and expense are required to venture outside our very beautiful home. Second, the evidence so far from exploring the solar system is that none of the other planets is hospitable, for a variety of reasons, and there is no clear evidence of life's past presence on any of them. Third, the craving to know *whether we are alone* really has deep spiritual significance, since it conceals the deeper question, whether to accept or reject God's claim on human beings as Lord over history and creation. Finally, the dark side of human ambition is horribly manifest in absurd modern visions of exploitation of the moon, other planets, or even farther parts of the universe, merely to continue Cain's culturally-based alienation from God.[5] C. S. Lewis[6] has treated this subject more fully in a number of books and essays.

Psalm 8 establishes a *biblical anthropocentrism*. Critics who claim it is misguided or destructive ignore the emphasis on personal relationship to God that sustains it, a point we must discuss further. To keep on track we next need to explore Psalm 139, which treats the subject more fully.

PSALM 139

O LORD, you have searched me and known me! You know when I sit down and when I rise up; you discern my thoughts from afar. You search out my path and my lying down, and are acquainted with all my ways. Even before a word is on my tongue, you, O LORD, know it fully. You have beset me before and behind, and lay your hand upon me. Such knowledge is too wonderful for me; it is high, I cannot attain it.

Whither shall I go from your Spirit? Or where shall I flee from your presence? If I ascend to heaven, you are there! If I make my bed in Sheol, you are there! If I were to take the wings of the morning, or dwell in the uttermost parts of the sea, even there your hand would lead me, and your right hand take hold of me. Were I to say: 'Let darkness cover me, and the light about me be night'—even the darkness is not dark to you, night is as bright as the day: for darkness is as light to you.

For you formed my inward parts; you knit me together in my mother's womb. I must praise you, for you are fearful and wonderful. Wonderful are your works!

You know me fully; my framing was not hidden from you when I was being made in secret, intricately wrought in the depths of earth. Your eyes beheld my yet unformed substance; in your book were written every one of my days, when as yet none of them were.

How precious are your thoughts toward me, O God! How vast is their sum! If I seek to count them, they are more than the sands. And when I come to the end, I am still with you.

O that you would slay the wicked, O God, and that men of blood would depart from me—men who maliciously defy you, who lift themselves up for evil, in opposition to you!

Do I not hate those that hate you, O LORD? Do I not loathe those who rise up against you? I hate them with a perfect hatred; I count them my enemies.

Search me, O God, and know my heart! Try me and know my thoughts! And see if there be any destructive way in me, and lead me in the way everlasting!

Anyone who argues that God is not *at least* personal must surely be taken aback by this psalm, since there's no mistaking what the poet says. Here the claim of Psalm 8 that God especially cares about human beings is developed and reinforced in an intensely personal way. From the standpoint of a scientific interest in creation, the focus on *biological* existence is particularly important. From the Greek or Roman perspective the body is a prison, limiting the boundless aims of the human mind and spirit; for the Hebrew, it is awesome and precious in its complexity and fragility. In particular, the poet couples a recognition of human mortality with the care and interest God has given to his development as unique even before his birth—"while I was as yet unformed." The issue entailed is not mere biological existence, but the fact earlier established by Psalm 8: that human life is eventful and given meaning by God's interest in us—"you knew all the days prepared for me, before they happened."

Such understanding exposes modern culture's attempt to identify an unborn baby as a mere *fetus*—a stark blasphemy against the divine intent—and the act of *abortion*, as a deliberate defiance of God himself. Reflect for example on the fact uncovered by modern crystallographic studies, that the detailed molecular structure of fetal hemoglobin is slightly different from that of normal human hemoglobin. The difference is important: The concentration of oxygen in the mother's blood at which oxygen binds to *fetal* hemoglobin is slightly *less* than that at which it binds to the mother's hemoglobin. As a result, if there is an oxygen shortage in the mother's blood, the unborn child will get it first. After a baby is born, fetal hemoglobin is converted fully to normal human hemoglobin within the first 48 hours. I don't know whether or not this is also true of other mammals, but surely we can agree with the Psalmist that we are "fearfully and wonderfully made."

Hence, from a scientific viewpoint, this psalm challenges contemporary understanding of what the biological creation really *is*. Because we have been able to understand the natural world first in terms of its physical mechanisms and their orderly behavior—what we might call "fourth day stuff"—the belief that "biology is only a complicated extension of physics and chemistry" panders to human arrogance. The physics and chemistry of biosystems is only the beginning of understanding them.

Most of us have had moments of existential insight into our biological, bodily existence, and we can understand the psalmist's sense of wonder at its fragile complexity as *being*. However, an important aspect of such insight is recognizing that we share this fragility and contingency of being with the rest of the living creatures; that is why I argue the psalm as a whole is concerned also with biological existence. We who are self-conscious beings are uniquely able to give that insight a voice, to think and speak about it; and, if we follow the poet's line of thought, to grasp that creating it has been central to the creator's purposes. Modern existentialist philosophers (notably, Heidegger[7]) have pondered these same questions, especially the fact that my unique *self-conscious* existence is inextricably linked to my biological nature, no matter what I may choose to think about the separateness of each.

The important difference between the psalmist's response to an experience of our unique biological existence, and that of most philosophers, is his explicit recognition of the presence and intentions of God in relation to himself as a living creature. For him the only *intelligent* response is to acknowledge in the same moment his awareness of the presence of the God who knows him fully.

Commentary on Psalm 139 usually explores the moral dimensions of God's knowledge of us. However, the opening verses are not asking a moral question at the outset; rather they state the Psalmist's awareness that he is always in the presence of a living God. Francis Thompson's poem *The Hound of Heaven*[8] begins with the poet's feeling that he has reasons to dread God's attention partly on moral grounds, and describes the resulting conflict of his heart:

I fled Him, down the nights and down the days; I fled Him, down

*the arches of the years; I fled Him, down the labyrinthine ways of my
own mind; . . .*

But the psalmist is not thinking about that experience; instead he is expressing an important stage in spiritual consciousness, more like that
stated by Gerard Manley Hopkins[9] in his poetry. It is quite natural that
we each begin with the egocentric assumption that we are the knowing
subject and all the world is only an object of our knowledge; we see that
belief in the earliest stages of childhood. Only later do human beings
acquire an understanding that others are also endowed with personhood
in their own right. So the psalmist shows us that a normal step toward
spiritual life is to become aware of the presence and concern of God for
us; that for God, we are never out of *his* awareness. Since to begin with
we are not sure of divine intentions for us, this could be disturbing: The
universe I inhabit is not entirely of my choosing or presupposition, but
belongs above all to *another* who knows me completely. The issue at stake
here is not merely awareness of guilt, but a much more ambitious pre-
sumption of autonomy for the self. The French philosopher Sartre states
in his simplest argument for existentialist philosophy[10] that "there exists
no such thing as human nature, since there exists no God to create it," a
deliberate denial of reality, and insistence on autonomy instead. Sartre
correctly describes himself as a "Cartesian," since it was originally Rene
des Cartes' proposal to establish all knowledge starting from an existential insight: "Cogito, ergo sum—I am thinking, therefore I exist."

A crucial step in the Psalmist's reflection is his belief that God's thoughts
and plans for him are not merely beyond his understanding; they are
full of goodness and life, rather than malice or indifference. In reflecting
on creation, we must assert that this is the 'proper' relation of self-aware
creation toward its creator, a deliberate choice to set aside alienation or
indifference. I say this, not ignoring the classic statements of the problem
of evil, but in spite of their persuasive power. Contrast the bitter despair
expressed in Ecclesiastes 9:1-6:

*All this I laid to heart, examining it all, how the righteous and the
wise and their deeds are in the hand of God; whether it is love or
hate, man does not know. Everything in front of all human beings*

is futile, since one fate comes to them all: to the righteous and the wicked, to the good and the evil, to the clean and the unclean, to the one who sacrifices and the one who does not. As is the good man, so is the sinner; and he who vows, as one who shuns a vow. This is an evil in all that is done under the sun—that one fate comes to all; also, the hearts of men are full of evil, and madness is in their hearts while they live, and after that—they go to the dead. Still, he who is joined with all the living has hope, for a living dog is better than a dead lion. For the living know that they will die; but the dead know nothing, and have no longer any more reward—even the memory of them is lost. Their love, their hate and their envy have already perished; and they have no more forever any share in all that is done under the sun.

Psalm 139 is very different view of divine intentions is the result of an established personal relationship based on trust and the acceptance of God's sovereignty as right. No one gets there by idealistic contemplation, since we all have some experience of the real existence of evil in the world. Robert Pirsig's famous book *Zen and the Art of Motorcycle Maintenance*[11] takes a critical step toward acknowledging the real existence of a benevolent creator, since it argues (in Pirsig's discussion of what he calls *Quality*) that denying the reality of creation's order and value does *not* lead to peace; rather, peace requires coming to terms with its character and reality as *good* in the sense used in Genesis 1:31 about God's valuation of what he had made.

And at this point, the issue of God's moral character and our personal orientation toward it becomes crucial. God's generous decision to grant liberty and potentiality to the living creation certainly entails risk for both him *and* us. Self-conscious beings *may* choose to oppose his purposes and reject his commands (for a variety of reasons); these are summarized by the New Testament as "law-lessness" (I John 3:4).

All the same we are surprised at the psalmist's sudden outburst: "Do I not hate those who hate you, O LORD?" His taking sides against those who do evil and rise up to oppose God's will seems both gratuitous and self-righteous. Why this ferocity? I think it can be understood as a declaration of intent by a person aware of moral weakness and frailty. That becomes clear in the closing prayer: "Search me, O God, and know my heart! Try me and know my thoughts! And see if there is any wicked way in me, and lead me in the way everlasting!" The word translated "wicked" here means "harmful" or "destructive," emphasizing its incompatibility with God's good intentions toward creation. Correspondingly, his positive request is for God to lead him "in the way everlasting." This is wonderful, since *biological fragility* is the topic underlying the entire psalm! Finally, notice that the psalm begins with the awareness of God's perfect knowledge of us as biological creatures and as persons, and his loving intentions towards us; and ends by asking that a heartfelt alignment with his loving knowledge of us be the guiding principle for each day's journey.

PSALM 145

I will extol you, my God and King, and bless your name for ever and ever. Every day will I bless you, and praise your name for ever and ever. Great is the LORD, and greatly to be praised, and his greatness is unsearchable.

One generation shall laud your works to another, and shall declare your mighty acts. On the glorious splendor of your majesty, and on your wondrous works, I will meditate. Men shall proclaim the might of your terrible acts; and I (also) will declare your greatness. They shall pour forth the fame of your abundant goodness, and shall sing aloud of your righteousness.

The LORD is gracious and merciful, slow to anger and abounding in steadfast love. The LORD is good to all, and his compassion is over all that he has made.

All your works shall give thanks to you, O LORD, and all your saints shall bless you! They shall speak of the glory of your kingdom, and tell of your power, to make known to the sons of men your mighty deeds and the glorious splendor of your kingdom. Your kingdom is an everlasting kingdom, and your dominion endures throughout all generations.

The LORD is faithful in all his words and gracious in all his deeds. The LORD upholds all who are falling, and raises up all who are bowed down. The eyes of all look to you, and you give them their food in due season. You open your hand, you satisfy the desire of every living thing.

The LORD is just in all his ways, and kind in all his doings. The LORD is near to all who call upon him, to all who call upon him in truth. He fulfils the desire of all who fear him; he also hears their cry, and saves them. The LORD preserves all who love him; but the wicked he will destroy.

My mouth will speak the praise of the LORD; let all flesh bless his holy name for ever and ever.

This psalm is very different from the first three. It is formal, *i.e.* proclamation, song, or liturgy. It seems repetitious until we look carefully at the details in each line. One way of getting into it more fully is to compare the repetitions and look for small gradations or variations. Another approach is to reflect on the many points at which it seems to ignore the flagrant conflict created between its affirmation of God's care, and how we ourselves see the world around us. We know that not only men but other living creatures experience hardship, instant tragedy and death; does God *really* give all creatures, even those who look to him, "their food in due season, or satisfy their desires"? What about predators and prey in a complex ecosystem? The poet seems determined to assign the highest moral value to a creation we moderns more readily interpret in terms of Darwinian survival.

Many Christians try to avoid this conflict naively, claiming that predator/prey relationships and other aspects of the non-human biological creation involving conflict and death are a consequence of the Fall—*human disobedience,* they argue, has resulted in a new and evil pattern affecting every living thing. In support of this argument they cite God's "curse" on the earth "because of you" [Genesis 3:17-19].

The problem with this argument is its open conflict with scientific evidence. Predator/prey hierarchies and other aspects of biological interdependence in complex ecosystems have existed long before human beings appeared on earth.

I think a better approach is to *acknowledge* the conflict between the Psalmist's viewpoint and our modern one and seek a resolution. We may also ask, whether biological death has the same meaning for the non-human biological creation as it does for us. The underlying issue is addressed by St. Paul in I Corinthians 15:51-57, the famous chapter on the resurrection of the body: "The sting of death is sin, and the power of sin is the law" (15:56).

Philosophically, the death of a lettuce—or a tree—has no moral significance, except as it may represent failure of human stewardship for creation. Correspondingly, the Old Testament does not include plants in the roster of living creatures, but rather as food for their sustenance. We are not deeply concerned with the death of an insect, either, since we accept the collective role played by insects in the ecosystem as a whole. Concern increases as we appreciate the greater complexity and potentiality in a creature more biologically akin to ourselves, especially if a relationship of dependency and affection develops; for some people the death of a pet is as momentous as that of a fellow human. But even this concern is related to our sense of responsibility for them and for their value as sentient beings; it is *not* based on a belief that death has an intrinsic moral significance for *them*. We may tentatively conclude that *biological* death, as it occurs in predator/prey relationships and the general competition for food, does not have fundamental moral or spiritual significance. Human beings are a very different matter.

For myself a small step toward understanding Psalm 145 happened some ten years ago, when I was working on the sixteen acres of forest surrounding our home in northern Idaho where we used fallen timber as fuel. It was a hot day and I stopped to rest a moment, and then looked down in amazement at the astonishing variety of mosses, plants, insects, and other living things at my feet. My first impression was colored by scientific education, as I saw before me many vivid examples of prey/

predator relations, biological competition for survival, and so on. But since I have been interested in this question for a long time, my next thought was: "No—that's not all there is to it—what I'm really seeing here is God the Holy Spirit caring for the creation!" And there came a silent but very personal question: "Yes! —and do you know that you're the only sort of being out here who's capable of opposing my intentions?" I'm seldom given to mystical experience, but in this case the contrast between my own thoughts and immediate awareness of God's presence ("you know all my innermost thoughts") was quite clear. I was not doing ecological harm that day—in fact, the contrary—but I realized for the first time something crucial about human identity and vocation. It was not merely a refreshing break from labor, but an experience that gave life and delight to the rest of that day.

HOW CAN WE APPLY SUCH INSIGHT TOWARD RESOLVING THE CONFLICT PSALM 145 RAISES FOR US?

First, let us consider criticisms often made of the biblical teaching that human beings were created (male and female) in the divine image, and therefore have a mandated dominion in creation. According to White and some others[12], this idea, and the divine blessing in Genesis 1:26-28 giving humans dominion over the rest of the living creatures, has given rise to the belief that we are at liberty to exploit and expropriate the earth for our own uses. Some professing Christian faith certainly have expressed such views. However, this is a distortion of the whole picture given in Genesis. In the complementary account of Genesis 2, dominion over creation becomes *stewardship* and responsibility *for* it; and unlike the archetypical Pharaoh and his consort, Adam and Eve are to *cultivate* and *keep* the garden the Lord God planted for them in Eden.

The meaning of these two terms in Hebrew is significant. The first, *tend* or *cultivate*, is more accessible to modern understanding because we use it the same way today: To provide with room for growth as well as offer opportunities for nurturing and developing the potential and fruitfulness of that which is cultivated. In the broadest way this goal is implicit in what we call *creativity* in human community, *culture* in the best and proper sense: All the intermediate stages of enterprise in humanity's relation to the world are supportive toward that understanding. The biblical view that humans are *intended* to enhance the latent potentiality in creation acts as a powerful corrective to the notion acquired from Greek philosophical thought that nothing man makes or does can *improve* on what nature already is. Such belief impeded the kind of empirical exploration of the world that Archimedes initiated; instead, the idea that our human reason is enough to deduce the meaningful order imposed by a divine reason became the dominant conception of natural science for more than two millennia.

The second term, translated "keep," is much more subtle. Its meaning can be teased out by looking for other instances where it appears in the Old Testament. Many of these are highly personal, in relationships between persons; consider for example Cain's defiant and dishonest reply to God after he had murdered his brother: "Am I my brother's keeper?" Still other uses refer to God's personal care for those who love and trust him: For example, Psalm 91:11, "He will give his angels charge of you, to keep you in all your ways"; God's unmerited blessing given to Jacob in his dream at Bethel, Genesis 28:15: "See, I am with you, and will keep you wherever you go"; or the blessing commanded for Israel by the Lord, Numbers 6:24: "The LORD bless you and keep you." Generally, the sense is the idea of protecting, looking out for danger, and caring in love for the welfare of the object of such love.

Perhaps there is a mystical element in St. John's account of Mary Magdalene weeping at the tomb on Easter morning (John 20:14-16). She saw the risen Lord standing before her and mistook him for the *gardener*. He must have looked like a person used to cultivating and keeping.

Further exploring such ideas as the proper biblical response to our stewardship has been well developed in *Earth Keeping: Christian Stewardship of Natural Resources.*[13] The topic is well outside my competence.

Critiques of a Judaeo-Christian view of human beings as having dominion in nature are also not internally consistent. They place responsibility on human beings to be stewards for creation but fail to see that true dominion entails understanding of and responsibility for the domain entrusted. There's little evidence for a spontaneous development of such a sense of responsibility in most societies around the world; concern for preservation of the environment has typically run last in competition with short-term exploitation for immediate human need or greed, while worrying about the matter seems to be a particular preoccupation of Western culture influenced by Judaeo-Christian concepts of nature as God's *creation*. People who make environmentalism central to religious belief often embrace convenient elements of Buddhism or Hinduism. They fail to understand what these religions actually teach: That the self, and a focus on realizing its inner consciousness, are ultimate reality; and that the objectivity of creation, *or* the reality of suffering, futility and death, are only an illusion. But Psalm 145 openly confronts us with the tension between modern conceptions of creation as "red in tooth and claw," and its contrasting declaration that God is "kind, gracious and generous toward all that he has made."

Concerning this tension, St. Paul says in Romans 8:19-22: "the creation waits with eager longing for the revelation of the sons of God; for the creation was subjected to futility, not of its own will, but by the will of him who subjected it in hope; because the creation itself will be set free from its bondage to decay and obtain the glorious liberty of the children of God. We know up to now the whole creation has been groaning, as if in the pain of childbirth...."

We suggested earlier that biological death is not the issue. Instead, St. Paul is depicting a serene order of creation that can be restored only when human beings have been fully renewed in the image of God. Nothing in the creation itself required its "subjection to futility"; the apostle bases his comments on what the LORD said to Adam about the outcome of his disobedience, Genesis 3:17-19. It is important that we understand God's comments not as vindictive punishment, but as *foreseeing* what would unfold from human choices. This is elaborated in detail in the account of Cain and his descendants, away from the presence of the LORD, in the land of '*wandering*' (see endnote 5). God deliberately chose, not to destroy human beings, but instead to give over the innocent creation to them for all the destructive choices they might make; and this choice was made in *hope* of a future liberation from such bondage. The Old Testament prophets often describe the earth as so defaced by human beings that it would "vomit them up" or as "polluted and suffering because of you"—not simply as environmental concern but rather because the moral inequity of human behavior is manifest in just such consequences.

Then what shall we make of Psalm 145? We recognized earlier that Psalm 8 depicts an unfallen creation but focuses on human beings as the object of God's interest. Psalm 145 has the same serenity, but its concern is the whole creation. The LORD is the gracious King who meets the need and fulfills the desire of every living thing; human beings are the intelligent voice through which all creation offers praise and appreciation of a generous and loving God. God who answers human prayers and needs is seen through the lens of personal experience in his full relation as Creator to "everything that has breath," a topic of growing attention at the end of the Psalms. Above all, God is near and listening to all who call upon him in truth, and saves them; he preserves all those who love him; but "the wicked he will destroy." An alternate rendering is: "the wicked he sends to their doom." This is not focused on God's judgment as an object of concern; it is entirely matter of fact, as if everyone knows that persons with evil intentions and deeds are simply unable to survive in the renewed creation. It resembles the final references to the wicked in Revelation 20 and 21.

These reflections on creation psalms have a connection with important themes in this book. We are concerned with aspects of creation seen through the lens of modern scientific understanding, and in particular with the biological creation. Ultimately it is the character of the Creator, made manifest in his work, that concerns us, whether or not we endorse intelligent design *as science*. Our appreciation of God's character necessarily shapes our perspective on what we see, and how we interpret its meaning.

MARVIN R. WILSON

Marvin R. Wilson has taught Old Testament and Jewish-Christian studies at Gordon since 1971. Dr. Wilson's widely used textbook, *Our Father Abraham: Jewish Roots of the Christian Faith*, has been translated into Italian, Chinese, Korean and other languages. For a number of years, Marv worked as a translator and editor of the *New International Version* of the Bible. Recently, he contributed a major article to the *ESV Study Bible*.

I am pleased to reconnect with the important work of Dr. Thorson. Back in the early 1960s, I was minister to college students at a church in Cambridge, Massachusetts. This happened to be at the same time Dr. Thorson was teaching at MIT. He did much more than teach chemistry at MIT, however. Professor Thorson was an active Christian witness on the MIT campus. Most of the sixty students in my college group were new believers, brought to faith by their fellow MIT students. Many of these science students commented to me on how Professor Thorson was a positive influence and encouragement to them as they were becoming grounded in their Christian walk. As a young professor, Dr. Thorson exemplified for these students that one could be a highly respected scientist and also a deeply committed Christian. These same concerns, decades later, continue to inform the research, thinking, and writing of Dr. Thorson.

In this brief space I have been allotted to respond to Dr. Thorson's ideas, I must be selective in my comments. Dr. Thorson raises many rich and intriguing questions for consideration. I plan to pick up on some of the specific points he raises; I also wish to make some overarching observations on how Christians might approach questions dealing with the intersection of science and Scripture as we move forward in this conversation.

At the outset of this response to Dr. Thorson's chapter titled, "Four Creation Psalms," I wish to express my appreciation for the thoughtful and integrative approach he has taken. Personally, I find Dr. Thorson's discussion of these Psalms very stimulating, balanced, and insightful. I think he and I are in principal agreement that the main purpose of Scripture is to teach us about God, not the methods of science. While God inspires the human authors of Scripture and gives their words divine trustworthiness, the authors are not scientists; their theological teachings primarily reflect the cultural context, vocabulary, and life setting of their world. Accordingly, the biblical writers are usually far more concerned with questions of the theological Who? or Why? than the scientific How? or When? I strongly concur with Professor Thorson that we must learn to "read and understand the Old Testament as Scripture for its own sake."

Indeed, the Psalms, in particular, have a lot to teach us about how one might reflect on the Creator and his works. After all is said and done, it is the theology of the Bible that is authoritative. In Bible times, one day in every seven was set aside to remember God as Creator and Redeemer (Exod. 20:8-11; Deut. 5:12-15). The Psalms are majestic in what they have to say about the King of the universe, an invisible yet personal God without whose power nothing came into being. These creation Psalms become for us striking, poetic models of personal spiritual expression, revealing to us ways of understanding God and his world. It is a truism, "If the Bible is God's Word, nature is his other Book." Indeed, as our presenter has eloquently emphasized, "The heavens are telling the glory of God" (Ps. 19:1). Paradoxically, though silent, they speak.

In his commentary on Psalm 19, I was positively drawn to the contrast Dr. Thorson makes between the Hebrew view of knowledge and that of the Greeks and Romans. This, I believe, is a key to understanding a biblical perspective on creation. The Hebrews often expressed their thoughts with a concrete or physical sense of perception, often employing descriptive word pictures. Further, they tended to emphasize experiential knowledge tied to this world. Their understanding of wisdom was largely empirical, rooted in real-life situations rather than relying on abstract concepts or vague ideas. At their core, the Hebrews were storytellers—and nature tells a story. The Hebrews conveyed this story primarily by lavish songs of praise directed to the Creator for his works.

The Babylonians and Canaanites thought of deities and nature as co-eternal. The Hebrews, however, were not dualists. God was not synonymous with his creation, neither was matter eternal. Thus, in biblical theology, nature always points beyond itself—nature is not God; a clear distinction is always made between the Creator and his creation.

In Dr. Thorson's discussion, I also resonated with his emphasis on the need to have a sense of awe and wonder in regard to nature. I think this is a fruitful area to develop further. In my reading and research, I have particularly found the writings of Abraham Joshua Heschel to be especially valuable in expounding this theme. Citing sources in the Hebrew Bible, Heschel points to the importance of cultivating a sense of mystery, awe, grandeur, appreciation, radical amazement, and the ineffable, all critical concepts, he believes, for connecting humankind to this personal God.[14]

In this vein of wondrous appreciation, Dr. Thorson focuses on Psalm 19 to make the effective analogy of enjoyment and appreciation of the stars and sun of the *natural* firmament *above* to that of appreciation and reverence for God's "*moral* firmament" *below*. As Psalm 19 concludes, I could not agree more with the emphasis of Dr. Thorson that "Christians must not see the gospel as something that ignores Torah" but as something to be revered and meditated on and obeyed from the heart. Indeed, this last point Dr. Thorson makes is, in the mind of the biblical authors, the key theme and lynchpin that holds the Law, Prophets and Writings together (Josh. 1:8; Ps. 1:2). To be sure, the creation account of Genesis is the very entry point into the Torah.

In Professor Thorson's commentary on Psalm 8, I was drawn to his emphasis on how important man is to God. Indeed, in the psalmist's words, man is made "little less than God" and crowned with glory and honor (v. 5). Some interpreters, fearing any description of human beings as too

"God-like," have sought to trivialize humans or deem them but puny and insignificant beings next to God. To God, however, man is an icon, a representative of the Divine. I think Psalm 8 likely echoes Genesis 1:29, "in the image of God he created him." While man is not God, he is like God in that he bears dignity, value, and honor. I think Dr. Thorson is correct in suggesting there is a *"biblical anthropocentrism"* established in Psalm 8. Yes, man's fall into sin has marred and sullied that divine image. But the Bible is more than a Book about God; it is also a book about man—not simply his plight, but also his potential. It is the story of his call as God's servant and representative to practice what Heschel terms, "sacred humanism." When our fellow humans are treated as "the work of God's fingers" (cf. 8:3), then something sacred will be at stake in interpersonal relations. Accordingly, to dehumanize another is to diminish the divine image in the world.

The final "creation Psalm" discussed by Dr. Thorson is Psalm 145. I am particularly drawn here to his description of an existential moment in his own life that deeply impressed him with the uniqueness that each individual carries regarding identity and vocation. In short, humans are the only sort of being capable of opposing God's intentions. This brings him to a discussion of stewardship and the choices we have to exploit or care for and wisely use the created order entrusted to us.

In regard to stewardship, Dr. Thorson calls attention to the meaning of the two important verbs in Genesis 2:15, the passage in which Adam and Eve are to *"cultivate"* and *"keep"* the garden given them by God. In regard to the verb "cultivate," as stewards for creation, he emphasizes "humans are *intended* to enhance the latent potentiality in creation," providing room for growth and developing potential for fruitfulness (p. 22). I would suggest the verb used here, *abad,* "to work," or "to labor" may hint at something even deeper. The late George Foot Moore, professor for over twenty-five years at Harvard University, points out that this Hebrew verb has a double meaning, embracing two actions that are normally viewed as mutually exclusive or contradictory to each other: work *and* worship.[15]

Largely from this verb, *abad,* the rabbis expounded the concept of "work as worship," that every area of life is God's domain and that there are no "non-sacred" occupations. What one does with the hands is no less sacred than the activity of the mind. In short, the dualism of Neo-Platonists, Gnostics, and others was avoided that mainly held physical labor in distain; it was deemed degrading. Yet the Psalmist declares to the Lord, "The heavens are yours, and yours also the earth" (Ps. 89:11; cf. Ps. 24:1). It seems God called human beings to do more than cultivate the earth. We do not worship the earth. But, for the believer, stewardship of the Lord's earth and its resources should hold a consciousness of accountability and of service to the Creator rather than exploiting creation at will. The very act of work, itself, was intended to be, as it were, an act of worship. In the words of Paul, "Whatever you do, work at it with all your heart, as working for the Lord, not for men" (Col. 3:23).

A few final observations as I draw this response to a close. First, Dr. Thorson has graciously modeled, with integrity, respectful conversation concerning issues of science and faith. He is a scholar who takes his personal faith seriously and science seriously. That is precisely why this conversation is so important.

Second, many of us will continue to have unanswered questions about the exact relation of science and Scripture. This is precisely why all Christians ought to have a theological "back-burner" on which issues may be left to simmer for a while. Whatever our view, we must not polarize, demonize, or become embattled. We must embrace each other in sincerity and graciousness in ongoing, thoughtful, informed conversation.

Third, part of our collective problem is that the Bible may be misread or misinterpreted. But science, too, sometimes changes its conclusion because of new data or new discoveries. No discipline—including science—is equipped to prove or disprove the Bible. When a Christian makes the statement the Bible is the Word of God, one is making a faith statement, but a statement based on meaningful evidence.

Fourth, both theologians and scientists must admit they are fallible, have assumptions—if not biases, have incomplete knowledge, and are part of a work in progress. The easy appeal, however, to the "God of the gaps," increasingly leaves many thoughtful Christians with an uneasy conscience.

Last, as we proceed, we must sincerely listen to each other, examining presuppositions and the data used to arrive at what is taught in each of these fields. In a spirit of humility, modesty, and charitable orthodoxy, we must continue to move ahead with the belief that science and faith are not incompatible or irreconcilable disciplines. Rather, we must persevere believing truth is ultimately one for those who put their trust in the Creator of heaven and earth.

CHAPTER 3:

FOURTH DAY THINGS

To whom then will you compare me, that I should be like him? says the Holy One. Lift up your eyes on high and see: who created these? He who brings out their host by number, calling them all by name; by the greatness of his might, and because he is strong in power, not one is missing.

—Isaiah 40:25-26

INTRODUCTION

The debate over intelligent design in biology has preoccupied many people concerned with Christian apologetics. As a Christian, and as a scientist trained in chemistry, physics and mathematics, I am concerned that Christian apologetics be soundly scientific in its claims and content. I am convinced that intelligent design is not a legitimate scientific hypothesis, and have argued in previous written work that *methodological naturalism* is an important presupposition of all the natural sciences—including biology. The basis for my argument is historical: The modern sciences of physics and chemistry (in the latter case, implicitly) began in the latter half of the seventeenth century, with the work of the "British empiricists." These men were committed to Christian belief. Yet they argued for naturalism as a *methodological* approach to scientific inquiry, which they thought of as "natural philosophy." In this chapter I discuss the historical tradition established in physics ever since—in order to explain why I think it is also appropriate to biology as a natural science.

THE PHYSICAL SCIENCES AND THE NATURAL SCIENCES

Genesis 1:1-2:4a is the first of two complementary biblical creation accounts. Creation's work is done in two sets of three days. In the first three, distinct realms are established by *dividing*: day from night, heaven from earth, seas from land. In the second set each is appropriately populated, following the order established by the first set.[1] On the *fourth* day, the sun, moon and stars are created.[2]

By "fourth day things." I mean those natural sciences not dealing directly with what we call "life sciences." For the sake of brevity, I call them the *physical sciences*—physics, chemistry and those applications of them to observational disciplines such as astronomy, geology, seismology, and so on. Specifically excluded from this narrower group are sciences that are broader discourses about "nature" (*i.e., creation*) more generally. In particular, biology and many aspects of the biological sciences are obviously natural sciences—but are excluded from the "physical sciences" as I use the term here. I think the distinction is justifiable philosophically, and it would have been clear to early physical scientists like Robert Boyle and Isaac Newton.

However, the distinction matters here, for two rather different reasons. As a chemist/physicist by training and experience, I became aware early in my career of the sweeping claim made by theoretical physicist Paul M. Dirac (and repeated by many other physical scientists) that biology and all other aspects of natural scientific inquiry may be seen as *trivial sub-consequences of the laws of physics*. As a young physical scientist I would have shared that view—which I now think a bit naïve. However, the idea is embedded in tacit presuppositions held by many people in the scientific community.

The second reason the distinction is relevant is that it has been *made so* by people who advocate intelligent design as the proper scientific explanation for uniquely complex features of the creation addressed by the biological sciences. While many ID proponents will argue in principle that their concerns also apply to claims of the physical sciences about cosmological origins (*e.g.*, the standard cosmological model or "Big Bang" theory), in practice their arguments are directed toward a sharp distinction being made between biology (where most argue substantially for ID as a scientific policy) and the physical sciences (where they have *not* actually done so). That's why we need to understand the tradition of methodological naturalism in science—and its origin in the rise of the physical sciences in the sixteenth century.

THE HISTORY OF PHYSICAL SCIENCE IS A BIT WEIRD

Since its beginning in the sixteenth century, novelty in physics has often been stimulated by celestial observations. For Galileo, seeing Jupiter's moons revolve around the planet suggested the analogy to the sun and its planets, as a confirmation of some more fundamental physical principle common to both; this intuition was reinforced by his observation that like our own moon, the planet Venus exhibits phases in its motion around the sun. When Kepler showed (based on the painstaking observations of Tycho Brahe and himself) that the orbits of the planets are not circles, but ellipses with the sun at one focus, a further sense that something more universal must underlie such complex mathematics resulted. The old idea received from Aristotle that heavenly and earthly motions are fundamentally different never recovered, and it remained for Newton in the late 1600's to establish the "universal" laws of classical physics valid in both the heavens and the earth. In the eighteenth century and later, discovery of additional planets unknown to antiquity further confirmed our confidence in the validity of classical physics—a confidence shaken only in part by the discoveries of modern physics (relativity and quantum mechanics). In the late nineteenth and early twentieth century, it became clear from better telescopes that some objects previously lumped together as "nebulae" (literally, *clouds*) were really galaxies of myriads of stars, and that our own "Milky Way" system was only one among myriads of galaxies; this led in turn to the beginnings of understanding about the origins of stars and the nuclear processes by which they shine—a physics that proves to be intimately linked not only to the most fundamental particles of matter and their relation to radiant energy, but in the end gives us a reasonably good account of the physical origins of the universe.[3]

But such grand-scale pictures aren't all. Recently, the astonishing dynamics of Janus and Epimetheus,[4] the co-orbital moons of Saturn, provides a nice example. The first clear observations came from the 'Voyager' mission's fly-by of Saturn in 1980-81, and have since been greatly augmented by extensive telescopic studies. Here's a layman's account: The two satellites, both constantly revolving around the planet, occupy orbits on an apparent collision course. Instead, at each close encounter they dance around each other, exchanging energy and angular momentum in the process; then Janus takes up the orbit of Epimetheus, and vice-versa, until their next meeting. A single cycle of the process (a double exchange) requires 4200+ orbits of each moon around the planet and ~8.01 years (earth time).

Any physical scientist familiar with the history of science since 1600 is fascinated by its annals of confusion and eventual discovery. My own commitment to science is compatible with Christian faith and understanding and indeed sustained by it, so I find a particular interest and meaning in these accounts. Many involved in the stories were believers in God—and their beliefs were relevant to their commitment to scientific enterprise.

Friends in Old Testament studies do not necessarily endorse my reading of Genesis 2:19-20a, but here it is anyway:

> So out of the ground the LORD God formed every beast of the field and every bird of the air, and he brought them to the man to see what he would call them; and whatever the man called every living creature, that was its name. . .

Sound exegetical interpretation of this text sees it as leading to God's creation of woman as a fit companion for man, who was otherwise *alone*; the meaning of the passage is that other living creatures weren't able to be fit companions. But there's much more there if we make the effort to look for it:

> *The LORD God brought the creatures to the Adam to see what he would call them.*

This suggests (a) God's interest and pleasure in the human response to what he had created, (b) his approval of the naming enterprise, and (c) the capacity of human intelligence to understand what was presented to it.

In the Old Testament, to give something or someone a *name* implies an authority with respect to it/him/her; in particular, it implies a kind of inner understanding of the true nature of what is named.[5] Hence "and whatever the man called each living creature, that was its name" is not a trivial claim; it ratifies the ability of the *Adam* to comprehend the true nature of creation around him—as well as asserting his legitimate calling to such a creative work.

In the context of modern thought, the *contingency of creation* and the *necessity of empirical knowledge* as the basis for understanding the world are also implicit in this short passage. The scientific revolution was the result of a long process of thought about the nature of created things, going back to the Medieval period; it is historically naïve to suppose that it took place spontaneously, as many people think today.

The scholastic medieval philosophers following Thomas Aquinas argued about whether reason alone is sufficient to account for what exists (*rationalism*), while others argued a contrary view: That there is no necessary order in creation, and that all we humans are doing is giving things names (*nominalism*). William of Ockham was a nominalist and is famous today for "Ockham's razor," the claim that if a number of philosophical arguments are given to explain a thing, we ought to choose the simplest of these as the best. The extended argument between these two schools led to a position fusing the two, called *realism* (John Duns Scotus is often considered an early realist philosopher). The realists argued that the created order is rational, but its character cannot be deduced using reason alone, because it is a *contingent* reality. It does not *necessarily* have to be the way it is, but *is* what it is by the sovereign choice of God, who created it. In Genesis 2, when God brings the creatures to the *Adam* to name, this extended philosophical argument is nicely captured for me. *Adam* could not use his reason alone, but must examine and experience each creature before he could name it properly!

While we may interpret this short text as God's authorization for every legitimate human creative activity, I take it here as a biblical endorsement of scientific enterprise in particular. God's *interest in* and *attention to* Adam's naming activity gives it significance, value and historical objectivity. To develop this claim fully would lead us toward constructing a more biblical philosophy of science.

However, the issue here is less abstract and closer to my personal experience of scientific inquiry. It is nicely illustrated in the words of Johannes Kepler when he had worked out the mathematics describing the orbital motions of the planets, expressing his joyful wonder that *God had waited centuries for a man to contemplate his work.*

It seems to me that at many points in the unfolding story of physical science something like Kepler's wonder at the incredible beauty and order of creation must certainly have been important to those involved. A wonderful moment was when James Clerk Maxwell realized that the electromagnetic field equations now named after him were not derivable from Newtonian dynamics, but described an *independent physical reality*. His classic second paper on electromagnetic field theory was treated at first as "metaphysical speculation" by one prominent scientific contemporary (Lord Kelvin); but Maxwell was really taking first steps toward the framing of modern theoretical physics. Einstein remarked at a commemoration of Clerk Maxwell's birth centenary in 1929 that had Maxwell not died of cancer shortly after his work on electromagnetic theory, he would probably have discovered special relativity. One of the simplest demonstrations of special relativity is obtained if one requires that Maxwell's four field equations retain their elegant mathematical symmetry in differently moving frames of reference; special relativity theory's odd relationships between time and space come out as a direct result. However, time and space *here* do not permit us to tell more of these stories!

My concern is just this business about *God being interested* in Adam's naming enterprise. Again and again, there is an odd sense for me in the telling of stories about physical discovery that there is *indeed* an interested spectator, silent yet supportive in the whole business. You may regard this if you like as my particular foible or weirdness. Coming back now to the bit of weirdness that began this essay, the dancer satellites in the rings of Saturn:

(1) If you take the equations of motion first formulated by Isaac Newton, and apply them to the motion of these satellites, the thing can be entirely accounted for (perhaps relativity theory is needed for tiny details). Ref. 4 cited earlier does the math, though the authors of the paper use more elegant and powerful mathematical methods than Newton's simple equations provide.

(2) On the other hand, *no one in their right mind* would likely invent the dancers and their orbits from pure imagination. I recall the sense of "gee whiz!" wonder at an American Physical Society meeting back in the 1980's when the recent Voyager movie footage was first shown (unhappily I missed seeing the film then).

This may be weird, but it seems to me that a careful listener might just hear a voice whispering: *All right, guys, you're getting pretty good: NOW try this one!*

It is an interesting fact that in spite of such successes in mechanics, it has never yet been proven that the solar system, for example, is dynamically stable. No one should ever think that even the obvious puzzles of the physical sciences have been adequately explored.

A sense of enjoyment at playing the wonderful game of physical science was cultivated by some first-class teachers who shared their pleasure in it with us. I had the privilege of being a student in several classes taught by the late Richard Feynman. Though Feynman was not a religious person, he had a deep respect and love for nature's order and beauty, and like many other scientists of Jewish ancestry he probably came by that unconsciously from the outlook on the material world many such people imbibe from childhood: *Not* as mystery or as goddess, but as the creation of God.[6] As a teacher he had the ability to get us excited about the strange stuff out there in the physical world and to make us a bit sharper in seeing just *how* unusual it is.

METHODOLOGICAL NATURALISM IN THE PHYSICAL SCIENCES HAS THEOLOGICAL ROOTS

The policy of *methodological naturalism* in the physical sciences was first advocated in the late 1600's by people like Robert Boyle, Isaac Newton and other members of the Royal Society of London. While physical science and mathematics, its working language, have flourished and become much more complex since then, no convincing evidence has ever turned up to suggest that fundamental change in the naturalistic presuppositions for physical science is either necessary *or* desirable.[7] So far it has been vindicated by overwhelming evidence, not merely in experimental laboratories but in repeated applications to practical technology. It is totally unconvincing for anyone to deny the validity of physical science while relying on devices that use it in every aspect of daily life.

Practicing scientists respond to uninformed attacks on methodological naturalism in science in various ways (purely deprecatory responses aren't included here!). Some point out that *methodological naturalism* is just one of the "rules" defining the "game of science." We're free to decide whether the game should be continued, a different game begun, or all playing abandoned, but *the rules are the rules*. The argument may seem frivolous, but it implies that science is necessarily a limited discourse about the world, neither comprehensive in scope nor independent of a larger framework of supporting assumptions held by its practitioners.

Others may respond by saying, as we might of a machine: *If it isn't broken, don't fix it!* This is more seriously engaged, since it recognizes the objective value of science as constructive toward human goals. I like this response a bit better than the first. I heartily agree that *physical science isn't broken, and doesn't need fixing*; and that this obviously applies as well to applications of physical sciences to those specific phenomena and mechanisms found in living things. Since we're only discussing fourth day things in this chapter, I postpone asking the interesting question whether there's more to *biology* than that.

Members of an inner circle sharing a body of common knowledge and experience usually respond to external criticisms in the ways just described. A harder task, but one essential to wider human community, is to set about explaining how we got to our present shared understanding of the situation. That's what I intend in the rest of this chapter. As a physical scientist, I must state at the outset that my thinking is already committed to the legitimate grounds for scientific enterprise, just as Luther found his conscience captive to the word of God. Contemporary attacks on methodological naturalism manifest ignorance of and contempt for the long-standing enterprise science has become. Starting a crusade against methodological naturalism in the physical sciences is completely absurd, like Cervantes' Don Quixote tilting at the windmills.

Proper explanation requires us to make a historical journey, and ask why Robert Boyle and some others in the latter part of the seventeenth century adopted the "mechanical philosophy"—what we now call physical science.[8] Boyle's contemporary Newton was the greater genius in mathematical and physical thinking; but Boyle must be considered more astute philosophically and theologically.[9] He seems to have understood for the first time that a clear distinction between natural science and natural theology must be maintained. This was motivated in significant ways by his theological understanding of God's transcendence in relation to creation. Boyle's advocacy of the new "mechanical philosophy" (as he and others in the Royal Society described what we now call *physics*) recognized from the start that it was a *limited discourse*—one that requires more comprehensive world-views to sustain it and make it legitimate.

While Hooykaas[10] has given some account of Boyle's thinking about creation in his pioneering work, a much more complete study is presented by Klaaren.[11] To begin with, Boyle followed Francis Bacon in rejecting medieval philosophy because its reliance on Aristotle's doctrine of nature obstructed a practical and empirical realism about the world. However, he found more explicit reasons for this rejection in his theological understanding of divine sovereignty. For Boyle, the medieval view of *nature* as a kind of intermediate "vice-regent" between God and creation was at best *"a vulgarly conceived notion,"* and at worst *"an impious blasphemy."* He was deeply influenced by people who adopted *voluntarism* as a theological understanding of the relation between God and creation. Voluntarism understood the *ultimate* explanation of creation's phenomena as a direct consequence of the sovereign will of God. While we may not find Boyle's voluntarism adequate to theological understanding today, it is a healthy antidote to the creeping paganism evident in modern culture today. The reinstatement of "Mother Nature" as religious icon obviously arises from a deliberate rejection of divine sovereignty in creation. Christians today should embrace Boyle's critique of the whole idea.

Other ways of looking at the relation between God and creation were also critical of Aristotle's teaching, and had significant influence on earlier thinking about natural phenomena in the sixteenth and early seventeenth centuries. One such approach was a *spiritualist* theology of creation, advocated especially by von Helmont (see Ref. 11 for a full discussion), and Boyle briefly considered it as an alternative before rejecting it in favor of voluntarist views. It is important for us here because it represents an almost diametrically *opposite* view: Namely, that divine agency is manifested as a kind of active principle in *all* natural phenomena (this idea has some roots in medieval alchemy). It can still hold some attraction for people who wish to see God as literally implicated in ordinary everyday things, and is often hidden in some common conceptions of God's relation to the natural world.[12] Von Helmont argued that the differing behavior of gases, liquids and solids should be understood as the result of differing degrees of a spiritual principle, manifest in their physical properties; for example, the tendency of volatile liquids to evaporate into a gaseous or dispersed state arises from greater amounts of the "spiritual" element in such substances. Our language still retains a vestige of this idea when we refer to alcoholic fluids as "spirits" or (*archaic*) "spirituous fluids." Eventually Boyle was not satisfied with spiritualist theology of creation; I think something like the following line of thinking helps to explain why.

From a modern perspective, Boyle's crucial decision to adopt instead the 'mechanical philosophy' was *epistemological,* rather than *metaphysical.* While he understood divine sovereignty as the *final* explanation for events in the natural world, his belief in divine transcendence led him to the conclusion that God's agency in creation is *not* subject to mundane human scrutiny (this idea was earlier emphasized by Duns Scotus). I think Boyle decided as a consequence that a legitimate human discourse about the created order should be conducted on grounds that scrupulously *avoid* claims about God's agency or God's presence in explaining mundane events. Hence, a second discourse about creation is possible, one sharply discriminated from 'natural theology' because it deliberately intends to explain limited aspects of natural phenomena on grounds *other* than divine agency. Terms of reference sustaining any such discourse are made legitimate and indeed animated by a wider *theological* understanding. But the discourse itself aims to describe creation in "creaturely" or "natural" terms of reference alone. Hence the "mechanical philosophy" could never be understood as a *final* explanation of the natural world, but only as a *deliberately limited* one. A further result of this choice is that understanding the creation scientifically comes not from reason or first principles derived from theology or philosophy, but from empirical examination. The belief that such an order or "laws" exist in creation was of course a presupposition rooted in the belief that God's sovereignty over the creation was itself orderly. (Parenthetically, a sociological question arises: What is likely to happen to interest in scientific inquiry in a culture that *lacks* any idea of divine sovereignty?)

Boyle's crucial step must not be *misunderstood* in the same way as it was deliberately misunderstood by Deism and the "enlightenment" of the century following. Boyle's contemporary Thomas Hobbes taught a materialist philosophy in which the ideas of the mechanical philosophy are taken to be ultimate truths. Since such teaching sets aside any acknowledgment of *God* as ultimate, Boyle openly regarded it as *atheism;* and he is said to have opposed Hobbes' election to membership in the Royal Society of London on the ground that Hobbes was an atheist. Nor did Boyle subscribe to the eighteenth-century Deist view expressed by Alexander Pope in the famous couplet: *Know then thyself, presume not God to scan; the proper study of mankind is man.*[13] This kind of thinking was impossible for Boyle, since he clearly believed that the transcendent God had revealed himself to human beings by the grace of God in Christ, borne witness to in the Holy Scriptures. Here he followed Bacon's idea of the two books of scripture and of nature, each book open to be read and understood by humans.

It is even possible that Boyle would have endorsed the interpretation of Genesis 2:19a that I have offered as a paradigm for natural science. In particular, his belief in the *contingency* of the created order meant that the entire world lay open to discovery through human inquiry. In this conviction, he followed and was likely influenced by the earlier ideas of Francis Bacon, but in Boyle and his Royal Society contemporaries the decision to pursue the consequences of such belief by practical action using the "mechanical philosophy" was more explicit.

I do *not* claim that Boyle understood the distinction he made between theological and scientific discourses as an *epistemological* distinction; that would attribute to him a philosophical modernity ahead of his times. Yet the epistemological substance of the distinction was made by him and others who shared his interest in the mechanical philosophy. Boyle was the first true advocate of *methodological naturalism* in the physical sciences. Furthermore, it's clear that for him this 'naturalism' was only *methodological* rather than *metaphysical* or *philosophical* as it often can be in today's scientific subculture. Boyle's crucial decision to advocate the new "mechanical philosophy" (as he and others in the Royal Society described *physics*) was theologically based; he understood that it was a *limited discourse*, one that requires more comprehensive world-views to sustain it and make it legitimate.

This chapter has explained why I cannot agree with the general repudiation of methodological naturalism in science made by many people who argue for "intelligent design." It displays a monumental ignorance of the history of science. It encourages foolish people to regard scientific enterprise as an enemy of Christian faith. Notoriously, where argument based on notions about ID has become part of fundamentalist culture, it has been absorbed into more general repudiation of all scientific truth. That's why some critics in the scientific community are justified in saying that ID is "just a new form of creationism."

I claim therefore that if intelligent design proponents wish to make a serious argument, they must recognize that attacking methodological naturalism in *physical science* is bad history *and* bad philosophy. If they disagree with this claim, they should undertake a serious deconstructive critique of the physical sciences. The fact that no such critique has ever been presented strongly supports the arguments made here, and I predict that none will be presented in future.

On the other hand, if advocates of intelligent design *accept* my argument that methodological naturalism has been proven justified in the physical sciences, they still have an alternative gambit. They can argue that biology is somehow different from the physical sciences, and that the difference provides warrant for rejecting methodological naturalism in *biology*. My plan in following chapters is to examine that argument. I do not agree that intelligent design offers a proper approach to the scientific problem posed. I do share the view that in certain important respects, biology *is* different from the physical sciences. Where thinking about that difference might lead us (in relation to methodological naturalism and the scope of new scientific inquiry) still needs careful discussion.

CRAIG M. STORY

Craig M. Story received a B.S. from Gordon College, a Ph.D. in Molecular Biology from Brandeis University and did his Post-Doc at MIT and Harvard Medical School under Hidde L. Ploegh. Story's research interests have focused on molecular immunology. His graduate and post-doctoral work involved work on the mechanism of antibody transport across the human placenta, and the ways viruses trick the immune system to escape detection. He also worked in the biotechnology industry in the area of drug delivery using the body's own antibody transport system. Most recently, his research has focused on generating antibodies for diagnostic tools that can be used by the world's poor. Since his 2006 sabbatical, Dr. Story has been exploring the use of new micro-scale tools to greatly speed up the process of antibody discovery. He continues this research, collaborating with the laboratory of JC Love at MIT's new Koch Institute for Integrative Cancer Research.

I am thankful for the opportunity to be involved in this discussion, as I believe Dr. Thorson is raising some good questions. Questions of how the life sciences relate to the physical sciences go back a long ways, and yet they should be revisited, as our understanding of biology has exploded in recent decades. Dr. Thorson is approaching this question from the perspective of someone extremely well versed in the physical sciences, and someone who, like myself, has an abiding faith in the reality of God's existence and active presence in our lives.

Many or most of us present have had personal experiences where God has subtly or obviously influenced our lives. But what does that have to do with our practice of science? Working scientists experience a tension that may go unappreciated by the average man or woman on the street. We would agree that a follower of Christ should live lives marked and influenced by God's spirit at every level, and yet, when we go into the lab, we purposefully/ operationally/ practically remove the miraculous and mystery from our daily work and in explaining our laboratory results. We assume God acts consistently through the laws of nature. This is how science operates; this is one of the rules of science that has been so successful in the physical sciences, as Walter has noted, and I would also argue it has been so in the biological sciences.

The success of science relies on the regularity and predictability of what we call the Laws of Nature. Both Dr. Thorson and I agree that at a very deep level, God is behind these; the very existence of these regularities we call Laws depends on God. Dr. Thorson has affirmed the success of so-called "methodological naturalism" for the physical sciences (chemistry and physics), and raised the interesting question of whether such an approach is sufficient for biology. This question will be probed more fully by others in this volume, but I would like to offer some history of the field of biology as background to guide our thoughts on this intriguing question.

The history of biology as a modern science has been one of removing mystery; new technologies, based on well-understood physical principles, are developed and give us new ways to probe how cells operate. We have made discoveries that would have been unimaginable only a short while ago. We can now obtain the full three thousand million nucleotide-long sequence of an individual human genome in days. A high-quality genome sequence (with 30X coverage, for sequencing aficionados) was recently done on an extinct human-like species that lived approximately 50,000 years ago based on 40 milligrams of a fragment of finger bone. From the sequence, we can confidently assert that she had brown eye color—this is just the tip of the iceberg in interpreting the data.

For centuries, until around the early 1800's, people believed that living things had a literal "spark" of life within them. And this idea still lives on in the popular imagination. I recall my own personal amazement in around seventh grade learning that there were electrical signals that caused our muscles to contract. At that age, I had a very unformed vision of electricity somehow mysteriously sparking about in our bodies. Soon enough, I learned how this phenomenon was the result of waves of voltage-sensitive ion channels in the membrane of neurons opening and closing in response to changing voltages across the membrane. In college physics, I learned about how the membrane behaves like a capacitor, storing up a potential difference across the lipid bilayer. What seemed magical and mysterious had an electro-chemical explanation. Indeed, this continues to be the pattern in biology. I would add that such mechanical explanations do not diminish my amazement and wonder. On the contrary, for me they only add a deeper level of appreciation and fascination for God's universe.

The structural understanding of a molecule, DNA, that is responsible for the inheritance of genetic traits, was arguably the greatest single leap forward in our understanding of cell biology. DNA is capable of self-templated replication, yet is subject to modification from generation to generation. Such genetic variations arise through quite well-described mechanisms and provide the raw material, the variation in individual fitness, for selection to act. A key point is that the variation occurs *before* the selection; the organism's DNA cannot anticipate what needs may arise—however, if the organism is unfit, it will not pass on its genes, and will be a dead end. Differential survival is a ruthless and yet simple binary test of fitness.

So, the question that will be raised in this symposium is the following: How is biology distinct from the physical sciences, and are such distinctions real or merely an illusion? Clearly, there are aspects of biology that mark it as distinctive, but are these differences of a fundamental nature? Such a question could potentially be upsetting to a person of faith. If all aspects of biology are fundamentally explainable by the laws of nature, doesn't that remove the mystery and wonder? Does that mean that God has no role in the world? Does that mean Richard Dawkins is right when he claims that God is an unnecessarily cumbersome explanation for that which we can explain through science? Good heavens no! I would argue with Dawkins as others have that a physical explanation does not exclude God's activity.

By placing God's action into areas that we have trouble currently explaining, such as life's origin, we run into danger of inserting God into a gap. This is a precarious position to be in, when those gaps, as I have said, are narrowing. Exactly how God influences and upholds Nature is a deeper question, and is not actually the question we are discussing at this moment about biology's relationship to the physical sciences.

In closing, let me try to describe what I think is a major source of confusion about biology. I hope to show in part why biology may appear to be truly distinctive. The big idea here is that biological entities, things like molecular machines and DNA, appear to function a lot like man-made machines and systems; they have a purpose and really appear finely designed to carry out their functions. I believe confusion comes about because of our pervasive use of analogies to explain complex molecular phenomena. I think such analogies can be helpful and are actually necessary, but we need to remember what is *really* happening and remind ourselves it is likely that finely tuned structures can emerge from physical principles, even if we have trouble intuiting or imagining that such things are physically and temporally possible.

There are many examples in biology texts of functional, analogy-filled language: Signals are sent, molecular motors turn and manufacture molecular energy storing molecules, ions are pumped across membranes using this energy. DNA is spoken of as a code, like a computer hard drive containing information in the nucleus; it is life's instruction book, after all. These descriptions are all shortcuts that obscure the reality. In reality, we should remember that these cellular structures are, for the most part, linear chains made up of small numbers of building blocks that spontaneously fold in a highly unpredictable yet precise manner. This allows them to do something that no man-made machines (yet) do: They self-assemble. Furthermore, that glorious and important molecule,

DNA, does not represent information in the way a computer hard drive or a book represents information. In both of those examples, the information is abstract. When we speak of information with respect to DNA, we have to be very careful what we mean by the word "information." DNA information is not embodied in the sequence of bases, GATACA, but, most critically, it is this sequence that describes the three dimensional shape of the molecule. This shape then binds to other molecules with particular complementary shapes. The sequence of nucleotide bases is really shorthand for describing the three dimensional shape of this molecule. At a most basic level, DNA has to be DNA—it is the molecular shape that defines it. DNA is not an abstraction. By thinking of DNA in this way, we can view it correctly as part of a complex system of interacting parts. Again, one that can self-assemble, replicate, and change over time. (By the way, this process is truly awe-inspiring to me.)

Describing cellular phenomena accurately boils down to molecule A binding to molecule B which then binds to molecule C and D, and so forth, and such an accurate description actually has very little meaning, so we give these molecules hard-to remember names and talk about the logic of their behavior. Yet, again, there do not appear to be any special laws of nature required to explain these phenomena.

Here is the problem: We start to view the molecular motors as structures that have formed in one instant, and forget the natural processes of molecule binding to molecule that led to their development and more accurately describes their behavior. To exist, biological structures must accomplish two interconnected goals: They must be able to replicate themselves, and they must function. This ability of self-replication, so clearly evident in living forms, has no counterpart in man-made functional systems, and currently, there is little evidence that anything is going on in the cell that could not in principle be explained with our current physical laws. Yet, keep in mind that out of such processes has emerged all of nature in its grandeur, including the unimaginably complex human brain. The relationship between the physical brain and the mind/person is one that is quite debated in philosophy and beyond the scope of my comments here; however, I believe it is really an area for

Christians to pay attention to, that is of far greater importance than the so called "evolution debate."

A biophysical and biochemical understanding of the brain and other complex phenomena is only one level of understanding, and as Christians we believe that there is more to us than our physicality. These mysteries will continue to be plumbed by philosophers, psychologists, theologians, sociologists and the like, in parallel with biologists. We need to remember that the physical universe is God's handiwork, and continue to explore the questions being faithful to God and the science. It's not "either or," but "both and."

CHAPTER 4:

CONTEMPORARY CULTURE AND EVANGELICAL SUBCULTURE

Thus the LORD, the God of Israel, said to me: 'Take from my hand this cup of the wine of wrath, and make all the nations to whom I send you drink it. They will drink and stagger and be crazed because of the sword which I am sending among them.' So I took the cup from the LORD's hand, and made all the nations to whom the LORD sent me drink it: Jerusalem and the cities of Judah, its kings and princes, to make them a desolation and a waste, a hissing and a curse, as at this day; Pharaoh king of Egypt, his servants, his princes, all his people, and all the foreign folk among them; all the kings of the land of Uz, and all the kings of the land of the Philistines (Ashkelon, Gaza, Ekron, and the remnant of Ashdod); Edom, Moab, and the sons of Ammon; all the kings of Tyre, all the kings of Sidon, and the kings of the coastland across the sea; Dedan, Tema, Buz and all who cut the corners of their hair; all the kings of Arabia and all the kings of the mixed tribes that dwell in the desert; all the kings of Zimri, all the kings of Elam, and all the kings of Media; all the kings of the north, far and near, one after another, and all the kings of the world that are on the face of the earth. And after them the king of Sheshach (Babylon) shall drink.

—Jeremiah 25:15-26

JEREMIAH AS CONTEMPORARY

This text from the prophet Jeremiah is relevant to our culture and to concerns of this book. Others could be used: Passages of burning condemnation for the society he is living in; historical accounts of good and bad behavior in the last years of the kingdom of Judah; a culture torn between gross idolatry, anxiety and fear about the future. There are brief sketches of individuals who see the future clearly but still choose righteously: Baruch the son of Neraiah, who stood by Jeremiah through thick and thin; unnamed leaders in Judah who risked the king's anger to save the prophet from dungeon and death. In personal dialogues of Jeremiah with the LORD, he struggles with his heavy task of telling truth to people who won't listen, yet intercedes with God for them even when God says *he* is not listening and will not answer the prophet's prayers. Some passages are filled with hope and extraordinarily specific promises for the future: In Babylon, an aging Daniel (9:1-2) learns from reading Jeremiah that the exile would last seventy years and intercedes with God to bring about the promised return. Baruch's brother Seraiah, going with the exiles to Babylon, is instructed by Jeremiah to stand on the banks of the Euphrates opposite the great tower symbolizing Babylon's glory, and read out the scroll of God's judgments against it (Jeremiah 50:1–51:64)— a solitary, utterly powerless Jew, invoking the promise of the living God.

The text above foretells precisely the historical events that soon followed Jeremiah's words, dead on target. This was the *entire world* within the horizons of the kingdom at Jerusalem. The prophet says nothing familiar will remain, but that God will also judge the destroyer nation.

Most remarkable are the character and staying power of the prophet himself. Often depicted as aged, Jeremiah was a young man when called by God, and he lived a very long time. He lives to see Jerusalem's destruction fulfilled in terror; Lamentations tells us how he feels. Nebuchadnezzar, knowing how accurately Jeremiah had predicted Babylon's hegemony, mistakes prophecy for politics; his officer Nebu-zaradan offers the prophet a secure situation in exile (40:1-6). Instead Jeremiah chooses to stay with the impoverished people left behind and endures the turmoil caused by guerrillas rebelling in a lost cause. Asked for God's counsel in view of Babylonian reprisal, he warns the guerilla leaders not to flee to Egypt and tells them God will deal severely with those who persist in idolatry. The last we read, he has been taken to Egypt by the fugitives and is still speaking the word of the LORD in their defiant faces (43:1–44:30). What an extraordinary life!

PARALLEL IN MODERN CULTURE

Like Jeremiah, people who worship the God of Israel today have a strong sense of the finality of divine judgment on contemporary culture, which has lost any sense of accountability to truth and righteousness. For people generally, many leading confused lives merely trying to survive economic injustice, growing contrast between haves and have-nots, and daily uncertainties as to old landmarks of law and morality, crime and punishment, this is a time of fear on every hand. As in Jeremiah's time, such confusion obscures faithful principles that can stabilize life. Popular media seem determined to "let it all hang out," willing to break every remaining norm of moral conduct. Political correctness replaces moral judgments based on harm done to persons, and while lip service is given to curbing destructive habits and passions, advertising openly encourages greed, lust, dishonesty and selfishness as norms. Idealists among our public figures seek to analyze or offer solutions for the detailed forms of *malaise* in human lives, or to find fit objects for blame. Few admit the terrifying truth: *We have met the enemy and he is us.*

Thirty years ago at the University of Alberta, some Christian faculty decided to create a monthly faculty forum where interested people could enter into solid academic dialogue about issues related to religion, ethics and culture. We did not intend to use the forum for Christian apologetics or mission, because we believed that should be left to individuals. We understood that few academics acknowledge either ignorance of or interest in such matters, since self-sufficiency and a misguided sense of importance are ruling principles in the academic world. Nevertheless a great many colleagues came to our first forum. J. M. Houston of Regent College spoke on the topic "*What is the most serious crisis facing our society in the next decades?"* Most on the steering committee expected Dr. Houston, a geographer familiar with worldwide issues of ecology/ environment/economics *etc.*, to speak on some topic linked to these problems. He surprised us, arguing that the most serious issue ahead for western culture would be the breakdown of the nuclear family, and that its effects would permeate all aspects of cultural, intellectual and economic life. His argument was well documented even then, and now we realize it was prophetic. Much human suffering in our time is traceable to this underlying cause; readers who know broken families will agree.[1] The recent (2011-12) "Occupy Movement" mass protests against corporate greed at Wall Street and in many other American cities seek to identify reasons why for many the "American Dream" no longer exists; media express puzzlement at the fact that while discontent is pervasive, few seem to know its real causes; above all there is a sense that the foundations of life are no longer secure.

Within our culture, those who believe in God feel the shaking of the foundations for evangelical Christianity as a subculture in it—for many of the same reasons. Somehow, profession of personal faith in Jesus Christ no longer has guaranteed consequences of reliability morally, financially or socially. The divorce rate is almost as high among those who claim faith as among those who do not,[2] and some even see no problem for faith in the live-in style of non-Christian contemporaries. Children are growing up with mothers and fathers who fail to parent them with enough love and attention, though money is seldom lacking. Profession of faith is not necessarily a guarantee of honesty in business, since many adopt the loose rules of culture dictating what has to be done for success in the chase for the brass ring. Partners in many Christian marriages struggle because they fail to grasp soon enough that marriage is not about changing my spouse but changing me.[3] Moral habits are more often shaped by the media than by the righteous divine principles that bring life and true character stability to people.

However, my intent is not to utter a "Jeremiad" over our society and its decline. I have a narrower concern: Things less obvious, but still important. The Old Testament critique of idolatry is not aimed at the vulgar desire to own things, personified in worship of the Baals, or at the immorality and unlicensed sexuality personified in the female goddess Ashtoreth, or at the insane cruelty kings and other rulers practiced in sacrificing their own children to Moloch the god of status and power. [Concerning these depravities, God said to his people: *I did not tell you to do any of these things, nor did they even enter my mind.* (Jeremiah 32:35)].

Instead the Old Testament says: First, since idols are created by men, they are unable to hear prayer, or to deliver people from oppression, distress and evil. Only the living God can do that. Second, idol worship is obviously blind-stupid, a failure of normal human intelligence. Isaiah's critique (Isaiah 44:9-20) stresses this second point brilliantly, concluding: "He feeds on ashes; a deluded mind has led him astray, and he can neither deliver himself, nor say, 'Is there not a lie in my right hand?'" Some have claimed that here the prophet is naïve, since pagan idols were not literally worshiped, but rather the "spiritual principle" they represented for sophisticated worshippers. But this is the heart of the matter. God says through Isaiah that the entire program of belief is (a) self-created, hence no such "god" can deliver or hear prayer; it is also (b) a failure of God-given intellect.

In responding to such ideas of "spirituality" we must recognize that modern usage of the word claims the same sophistication attributed to ancient pagans in their cruder idolatries and is, therefore, also a failure of human intelligence. While materialist atheism based on "the scientific world-view" cannot answer the deepest questions human beings ask, at least it openly denies that such "spirituality" is anything other than fraud.

Ignorance (and inability to recognize it) are the particular marks of contemporary cultural decay that concern me here. Trivial evidences arise everywhere and every day: Journalists and other media persons unable to write or speak clearly or grammatically, often failing to understand the historical background of current events; people who have no idea where age-old metaphors like "the handwriting on the wall" originated or even what they really mean. The "dumbing down" of graduates from educational institutions at all levels is now widely recognized, though not perhaps appreciated for its full effects. But ignorance has long been a secret *virtue* for modern culture, especially in North America. As a science teacher, I often found that even very capable and successful students did not really care about truth for its own sake, but only as a pathway to power and affluence. Once these latter aims are attained, people are often satisfied not to know more about reality, and correspondingly, will consider the pursuer of truth to be a naïve person. All this is well known as long characteristic of American society; unplanned consequences when the dream has died are less obvious.

To the extent American evangelical Christianity partakes in the norms of broader American culture, it not only shares in the grosser vices depicted earlier, but equally shares its ignorance. If Christians are to be adequate critics of modern idolatry and foolishness, their apologetic arguments and their presentation of what is true either biblically *or* scientifically cannot afford to be trivial or naïve.

NONSENSE ABOUT ORIGINS

One index of modern cultural collapse is widespread propaganda by people who use scientific achievement or their status as participants in it to support a particularly aggressive form of atheism. Their arguments often center on claims about scientific accounts of origins in the physical sciences and biology. Since our understanding of physical origins of the universe and the earth is on relatively firmer grounds in the "Big Bang" scenario (what scientists call "the standard cosmological model") and in growing knowledge about planetary systems in stars, argument about physical origins has a clearer foundation; as a result, recent-earth creationism is now losing favor with many evangelicals. Ronald Numbers' excellent book *The Creationists*[4] lays out the whole history of the movement, including Numbers' own personal experience growing up in Seventh-Day Adventist society.

Over the years I have gotten a few scars myself as I ventured into the "no-man's land" contested by adamant creationists and strident atheists. The role played by the American Scientific Affiliation under its early leadership and more recently with Bob Herrmann has been one of the few bright spots in the past fifty to sixty years, keeping evangelical thinking about science soundly accurate.

Yet biological evolution remains an active gambit for aggressive atheism, and a major target for evangelical Christian attacks. That is why the intelligent design movement has gained so much attention from evangelicals.

When Robert Jastrow first published *God and the Astronomers*,[5] the evidence that (a) our physical universe had originated in an explosion of light energy at a single point, and that (b) space-time has since unfolded outward from that beginning, led many scientists like Jastrow to acknowledge their surprise that this extraordinary "beginning" was reasonably documented by the facts. Among astronomers who were my acquaintances during student days at Caltech, one or two have become Christians, in part because of this remarkable thing.

In the old center foyer under the dome at MIT, there was a large bronze plate with an antique quotation expressing earlier secular belief about cosmological origins. It began "Gross gravitating matter" and went on to explain something about the accretion of solar system matter influenced by gravitation. There is nothing wrong with that idea scientifically, but viewed from the standpoint of previous cultural tradition it offered a new version of "In the beginning." The plaque obviously dated the Institute's origins to a time when most scientists were yet unaware of the amazing future just ahead for modern physics. A century later, we *still* cannot quite fit gravitation into the models that accommodate almost everything else in unified accounts. But the old plate offers interesting reflections on the nature of science and the problem created by using it as society's prophetic voice. MIT has always been a secular place; but such secularism was complacent rather than aggressive.

Following Jastrow's book, others speculating about implications of the "Big Bang" for human self-understanding soon followed. Most offered various "cosmic" approaches for assimilating the new picture. Some evangelicals jumped to the conclusion that identifying the big bang with the opening verses of Genesis 1 was now a settled conclusion.[6] Few understood that such a convenient coupling has serious theological problems, since it presumes *a priori* that the aim of Genesis 1 is to provide (like the Gilgamesh epic and other ancient origins tales) an account of the technical *process* by which God created the world.

As the complexity entailed in the standard model's account of origins became clearer (fundamental particle theory and cosmology on the largest scale are intimately related to each other), the next stage of works popularizing what we now think about physical origins started to appear. Carl Sagan's *Cosmos*[7] and related media programs offered the meaning (or lack of it) for pagans, intoning in solemn parody of ancient Christian liturgical forms that "The cosmos is all there is, or was, or ever will be." Stephen Hawking's *A Brief History of Time*[8] gave more authoritative opinion, as he was deeply involved in work on fundamental cosmological theory. However, as time continued, he increasingly used his position to argue his atheism as if it were implicit in the science. In particular he seems to hold or have held the naïve belief that since his theory of the possible origin of many universes by spontaneous processes seems to have no need of any causative process such as a creator, one may conclude that no such creator exists.[9] His books and writing show a lamentable ignorance of history, philosophy or theological reflection, oddly reminiscent of early Soviet astronaut Yuri Gagarin's statement on return from space that he found no evidence of God there.[10] Given modern cultural ignorance, such aggressive marketing of atheism has a certain plausibility, and naïve people assume it is somehow supported by the science.

Fred Hoyle (1915–2001) was another cosmologist willing to offer speculative opinions on almost any subject. He received early recognition for his development (with Gold and Bondi) of the "steady state" or "continuous creation" model to explain the observed data for an expanding universe; by the 1980's, increasing evidence in favor of the "Big Bang" model moved him to give up the idea. An honest scientist will face the facts, and Hoyle's openness about changing his mind was an attractive aspect of his character. In 1957 Hoyle gave the convocation address at Caltech when I received my doctorate. He told his audience that an important reason he worked to develop steady state theory was that he disliked the implication of "Big Bang" theory that the universe had a beginning and hence there might be a Creator. Hoyle's admission shocked me, since as a young scientist I took great care to maintain integrity in scientific questions and never allow my religious belief to bias my thinking, and here was a famous man admitting that such bias was fundamental to his work!

Sometime in the 1970's I heard Hoyle lecture at the University of British Columbia on his interpretation of the Aubrey Holes at Stonehenge.[11] These three concentric rings of postholes are probably the oldest human artifacts at the site. Hoyle gave a convincing account of their possible use as holes for movable posts enabling prediction of solar and lunar eclipses: One ring marking motion of the sun during the annual revolution of earth around it; a second ring, motion of the moon in its monthly revolution around earth; finally the third ring, marking the motion of the *ecliptic line*. The ecliptic line is the (moving) intersection of the solar and lunar planes of revolution, and itself defines a third plane by its motion. Eclipses of the sun or moon may occur only when posts in the three Aubrey rings are all in a straight line, and this was likely a predicting device. It is very plausible that the earliest building at Stonehenge *was* related to a religious interest in predicting important events such eclipses, summer and winter solstices, and Hoyle's interpretation makes good sense. However, Hoyle ended his talk with a breathtaking absurdity: This, he said, is the likely origin of the Christian doctrine of the Trinity: The post for the solar position symbolizes the Father; that for the moon's position, the Son; and of course the third post, for the invisible ecliptic line, symbolizes the Holy Spirit! That a man well known for his knowledge and contributions to scientific culture should publicly exhibit such appalling ignorance of Western culture and history underscores my point about contemporary culture.

Hoyle made other pronouncements later in life. He became convinced that attempts to explain the origins of life (chemical evolution) and subsequent early evolutionary change cannot and do not work. He is famous for several statements:

(a) "The notion that not only the biopolymer but the operating program of a living cell could be arrived at by chance in a primordial organic soup here on the earth is evidently nonsense of a high order."

(b) Concerning random emergence of even the most primitive cell, Hoyle said: "This is as likely as that a tornado sweeping through a junkyard might assemble a Boeing 747 from the materials therein."

Since Hoyle believed that some intelligence from outside our solar system was responsible for life here ("panspermia"), he is sometimes credited with having given early *atheistic* support to the intelligent design movement. I am not sure that is a credit to the movement; in any case, Hoyle did not share the religious motivations of today's ID proponents. He was just a loose cannon in scientific culture—interesting, but not to be taken too seriously if profound cultural ignorance is a major concern.

Pros and cons of using biological evolution as a gambit for atheism are more subtle. Propagandists like Richard Dawkins[12] and Harvard biologist Richard Lewontin[13] have used their books and other media to argue that biological evolution eliminates any reason from biology to believe in a creator, or any sort of God whatever. Their success in this illogical argument is abetted to considerable extent by equally illogical evangelical responses: Persuasive evidence showing human similarity to other animals and common biological descent is rejected *a priori* as incompatible with biblical teaching about God and humans. Blatant atheist propaganda would have almost no effect today if evangelicalism as a subculture had not ignorantly chosen to resist factual evidence in biology as a conspiracy against Christianity. Nineteenth century evangelical Christians like biologist Asa Gray were generally much more sympathetic to Darwin's hypotheses about evolution than theologically less orthodox churchmen like Anglican bishop Wilberforce in his famous debates with Thomas Huxley.[14] Christians committed to the pursuit of science as a vocation must be willing to examine ideas of Darwin and others about biology purely on their *scientific* merits, even if they are not biologists by profession. It is a matter of intellectual integrity. Doing that, many of us have concluded that while Darwin asked a very good question about the origin of species and also gave some good partial or provisional answers, the account given by current theories is still incomplete *scientifically.* However, that certainly does not justify the response many intelligent design proponents give: "Here ends the explanatory power of science to account for what we see; and now we have to offer a theologically based account."

In an attempt to give creationist arguments space, some evangelicals writing or speaking publicly on science and creation have raised theological and philosophical caveats about the legitimacy and scope of scientific inquiry. Books and articles by Norman L. Geisler and others[15] claim a crucial distinction between "operations science" and "origins science" is necessary; they argue that scientific methodology may be legitimate for studying ordinary phenomena in the world *today* but has no competence to address questions about *origins,* whether in physics, astronomy, geology, or biology. It is unclear when or how a warning flag goes up to tell a scientist that a question lies outside his/her competence, but apparently Geisler *et al* are prepared to offer rulings. This argument is so clearly *ad hoc* and so patently absurd to anyone experienced in scientific practice, that it should embarrass any thinking Christian. The weakness of the case for intelligent design is exposed if its proponents appeal to Geisler's argument—as some do.

SUMMARY / PROSPECTUS

Evangelicals in North America, and in the wider world where their culture and teaching has influenced people, have generally failed to think deeply enough either about the world they live in, *or* the word of God they profess to believe and understand. They have been particularly willing to accept easy answers on subjects that demand serious intellectual struggle and inquiry. It will not do to rely on technology daily and yet affirm teaching about creation that flatly repudiates the truth of the physical sciences. It will not do to bring up young people with intellectually childish treatment of biblical material and then be surprised if they abandon Christian faith after taking university geology, biology, history, or philosophy courses. And it will not do to offer "reasons to believe" that cannot stand up in the marketplace of severe scientific and historical inquiry.

My aim is a serious critique of the intelligent design movement as evangelical Christian apologetics. I have already set forward the history and basis for methodological naturalism in the physical sciences (Chapter 3). This historical tradition is neither understood nor valued because of widespread ignorance in evangelical Christian subculture. Educated persons must learn more about scientific culture and history than a narrow expertise for their own professional work requires, even though that takes effort. Otherwise we are failing our fellow Christians. I am ashamed when other scientists, trained by experience and wider knowledge to appreciate scientific tradition and history, are exposed to this sort of ignorance on becoming Christians later in life. Some scientists I know personally are in just this difficult situation.

In the next chapter, I give a brief account of the intelligent design movement. Most ID proponents argue there is something different about biology—something physical science cannot explain—and they claim it *is* explained by the hypothesis. I agree that biology *is* different; I *do not* agree that ID offers a scientific approach to the problem. In the final chapter I offer some tentative comments on intelligent Christian responses to the theory of biological evolution on the basis of its current *scientific* merits.

KARL GIBERSON

Karl Giberson is an internationally known science-and-religion scholar, speaker, and writer. He has lectured at the Vatican, Oxford University, London's Thomas Moore Institute, the Ettore Majorana center in Sicily, the Venice Institute of Arts and Letters, the University of Navarre in Spain and at many American venues, including MIT, Brigham Young, Xavier, Stonehill, Wheaton, Gordon, the Harvard Club of New York and others. He has published more than 150 articles, reviews, and essays, both technical and popular, in outlets that include *USA Today, LA Times, Salon. com, Discover, Weekly Standard, Quarterly Review of Biology, Perspectives on Science & Faith, The Edge.org*, and *Books & Culture*. He has written or co-authored seven books, and contributed to many edited volumes.

EVANGELICALISM AND SCIENCE: WILL THERE EVER BE PEACE?

The *Chronicle of Higher Education* reported in the fall of 2012, just before president Obama's historic re-election, on a Pew study that found "only 9 percent of scientists self-identified as conservative, while 52 percent called themselves liberals." And "only 6 percent of American scientists self-identified as Republicans." This was an election cycle that will long be remembered for the consistent denial of mainstream science by Republicans; evolution, the mechanism of conception, and human-caused climate change were challenged at various times. On one occasion, a Republican congressman up for re-election called evolution and the big bang "lies from the pit of hell." (He was defeated.)

Pew also released a report at around the same time indicating that 80% of evangelicals typically vote Republican. This confirms the widely held perception that the Republican Party is the "Christian" political choice.

The point is obvious and electoral politics is only one lens through which to view it: Evangelicals and scientists are on quite different teams right now. Let me give you one more indicator of this striking divergence:

Despite their vast numbers, virtually no evangelicals have ever won a Nobel Prize. Bill Phillips is the closest to an exception at the moment. He shared the Nobel Prize in physics in 1997. But Phillips rejects the label "evangelical" and calls himself a Methodist. (I have seen a video of Bill singing with his church choir however, and he certainly looked like evangelical to me!)

In contrast to the situation with evangelicals, an astonishing 36% of the Nobel prizes awarded to Americans have been won by Jews. This is an extraordinary number that only becomes more remarkable when we look at the demographics—according to the Pew Forum on Religion and Public Life, only 1.7 percent of Americans identify as Jewish, while 26.3 identify as evangelical Protestants. That translates to roughly seven million Jews in the United States, contrasted with about 80 million evangelicals, or even more depending on where you draw the boundaries. 337 Nobel prizes have been awarded to Americans, as of this writing, and more than 100 of those have gone to Jews. One has gone to an evangelical. Let us think about how such a disparity arises.

Picture the children of these two communities—Jews and evangelicals—growing up in America. Somehow the evangelical child will, most likely, be raised with a distrust of science, a fear that it is incompatible with her faith. She will not be encouraged to pursue science as a Christian vocation. If scientists were invited to speak at her church, they are likely to represent a group that attacks science as "godless." When science topics come up in her Sunday school class they will be presented in opposition to what she is learning in high school. She will be unlikely to choose science as a career or, if she does, she will probably have abandoned her evangelical tradition. The child being raised in the Jewish home will hear science discussed respectfully and she will be encouraged to pursue it. She will be inspired that people from her Jewish tradition have won Nobel prizes, like Albert Einstein and Steven Weinberg. Her extended family will cheer her developing interest in science.

A widely discussed Barna survey looked at the reasons why young people are abandoning the evangelical church. The survey concludes that young people perceive the church as *anti-science* and this is one of the primary reasons they are leaving. My daughter left the evangelical church in which she was raised after being browbeaten with young earth creationism in her Sunday school class. My family had attended that church—the college church on the campus of Eastern Nazarene College where I taught for most of my career—despite the frustrating intrusion of right wing fundamentalism, especially around elections. The church was not fundamentalist but there was absolutely no willingness to confront fundamentalism—creationism, flood geology, literalism—when it arose. My older daughter remains within the evangelical fold but attends a local church that she and her husband think is intellectually impoverished when it comes to science. Their commitment is tenuous at best.

These problems are noted in the pages that follow. In particular, the culture war that has arisen over the question of origins is highlighted—the ubiquitous and perennial creation-versus-evolution debate. In this culture war, we find so-called "new" atheists like Richard Dawkins, Daniel Dennett, and Jerry Coyne arguing that evolution is incompatible with belief in God. This, of course, is exactly the same argument being made by evangelicals like Ken Ham, the late Henry Morris, and the fellows promoting Intelligent Design at the Discovery Institute.

The intensity of this conflict is all too familiar. Over the course of my quarter century in evangelical higher education at Eastern Nazarene College, I was continually assaulted by fundamentalists for being a heretic for accepting evolution, and my employers were enthusiastically encouraged—sometimes with financial incentives—to fire me. I spent many unhappy hours in administrators' offices at Eastern Nazarene College addressing the concerns of constituents—from groups with names like "Concerned Nazarenes"— who had proclaimed that they were the gatekeepers of orthodoxy.

This raises the important point that has become for evangelicals the elephant in the room, or perhaps we should say the "elephant in the foyer." Dr. Thorson notes—and I am quoting here because he said it so precisely—"Persuasive evidence showing human similarity to other animals and common biological descent is rejected *a priori* as incompatible with biblical teaching about God and humans."

By rejecting *scientifically persuasive evidence*—as a community of faith— evangelicals have avoided coming to terms with it. We have not invested the effort to develop an appropriate theological perspective. We have run off many of those who are trying. Westminster Theological Seminary ran off Peter Enns. Olivet Nazarene University ran off Richard Colling. Calvin College ran off Howard Van Till and John Schneider. Cedarville College just dismissed a professor this year for critiquing young earth creationism. Wheaton College forces their professors to sign a statement denying human evolution, despite overwhelming and *scientifically persuasive* evidence that it has occurred.

The energy that should be directed at these serious challenges from science has been diverted into a quixotic project to undermine the relevant science, or to make it so unorthodox that it cannot be discussed. Countless evangelical efforts—some funded to the tune of millions of dollars per year—have as their "ministry" the undermining of central ideas in biology and cosmology. These highly visible projects—like the creation museum in Kentucky run by Answers in Genesis— play right into the hands of the atheists. Such projects empower atheists to wield evolution as a club to bash religion, knowing that evangelicals are hearing an identical argument from their own leaders. The result is that many, many Christians abandon their faith when they learn that evolution is true—creating a most discouraging brain drain. Ronald Numbers, the world's leading historian of the creationist movement, Michael Shermer, president of the Skeptic Society, and E. O. Wilson, the founder of evolutionary psychology and one of the most influential scientists in the world, all lost their childhood faith when they discovered that their religious communities had misled them about evolution.

In summarizing this important issue, Dr. Thorson makes a statement that I *think* is true. I certainly hope it is true. He says "Blatant atheist propaganda would have almost no effect today if evangelicalism as a subculture had not *ignorantly chosen to resist factual evidence in biology as a conspiracy against Christianity.*" (The emphasis here is mine.)

The quarry in this book is origins and intelligent design. But, as our national discussion reveals—and Dr. Thorson makes clear between the lines of his specific critiques—the problem is much larger: It is science in general. He accuses evangelicals of having "*ignorantly chosen to resist factual evidence.*"

Tragically, the techniques used to persuade evangelicals to reject biological evolution are crude instruments that indiscriminately destroy the credibility of science as a whole and even the veracity of "facts." By presenting science as atheistic, as conspiratorial, as always changing its mind, as insular and self-protective, and as narrow-minded, concerns are raised about the entire scientific enterprise. What young evangelical wants to spend years getting credentialed to join a community of narrow-minded atheistic conspirators who don't make much money? These things matter and have practical implications.

In the 2012 election season, we witnessed the Republican presidential candidates—several who would call themselves evangelicals—rejecting evolution with a show of hands with only the fading-and-soon-to-be-gone Jon Huntsman dissenting and accepting evolution. If such views take over the Supreme Court—unlikely in the short term—we will find high school biology seriously compromised.

Human induced climate change is treated the same way, rejected by almost all evangelicals, despite having become mainstream science and posing serious challenges that need to be addressed. In fact, this topic produced some of the strangest anti-scientific comments we have heard in the past year; in ridiculing concerns about carbon dioxide being a dangerous atmospheric pollutant, both Rick Santorum and Paul Ryan suggested that we "make that argument to a plant"—remarks that many evangelicals cheered. Now plants, of course, need carbon dioxide to thrive, but the concern of climatologists is not that carbon dioxide has somehow become toxic to all life-forms, but that it is a greenhouse gas that traps heat from the sun and raises the temperature of the planet. Insurance companies are already demanding higher premiums to insure against coastal flood damage because the effects of global warming are both disturbing and clear.

Evangelicalism and science have, unfortunately, been drifting apart for a century. And, over the past few decades, both have been busily enlarging the chasm between them so there can never be a reconciliation. We have a serious problem and very little commitment to doing anything about it. Evangelical leaders like Walter Thorson, lecture series like the one on which this book is based, and evangelical colleges like Gordon and Eastern Nazarene that promote strong science are all efforts in the right direction. But such projects cannot compare to those that oppose them, like Ken Ham's Answers in Genesis, that spends millions of dollars every year warning evangelicals to flee from science.

CHAPTER 5:

A BRIEF HISTORY OF THE INTELLIGENT DESIGN MOVEMENT

INTRODUCTION

Any account of the ID movement requires a disclaimer by the person giving it, and (if it is to be *brief*) some clear limits on scope. Let me offer my disclaimer first. I cannot claim to make a final appraisal of the ID movement as though I myself stood *outside time*. I know many current advocates of intelligent design, some at least as acquaintances, others more familiarly because we have had extended dialogue both personally and in writing. My sympathy for their views is a very *critical* one—but is still a *sympathy*. Some ID proponents are competent scholars in their own right; some of their work is sound criticism of contemporary follies. It is certainly true that the theory of biological evolution is a kind of sacred cow in the scientific establishment—for many of whom attacking evolution is a kind of mortal sin.[1] Many ID proponents have been careful and fair in their discussions of evolution as icon, and I agree with much of their negative criticism—especially in relation to biological origins. Most are willing to give due weight to establishment views where these are credible and to respect sound scientific work where they find it. A few have waded in with their minds already made up on the issue of evolution; for a scientist that is never a good policy, but we have seen earlier that the same predisposition is not unknown among dogmatic opponents of Christian belief—whether scientists or not. Many authors whose work is discussed have examined the validity of their arguments and critical conclusions drawn from them. Although most are not professional biologists (Michael Behe of Lehigh University is a notable exception), negative critiques offered by some are recognized as fair by competent working biologists. I suggest that in part this reflects the incompleteness of current scientific understanding about biological organization, a topic I try to discuss in Chapter 6.

It is important for me therefore to repeat my disclaimer: I am not a biologist, but a *physical scientist*, and cannot pretend to understand all the technical details that properly shape a sound scientific judgment on the issues. On the other hand, I do know something about both the philosophy and history of science and am familiar with these almost as a second vocation. I also take encouragement from the thinking of a few other scientists who have been willing to move outside the box of their own professional specialties. Sometimes a view from outside reveals unusual aspects of the situation so taken for granted that *nobody can see the elephant in the room*.

That is why it is so important to remember that we cannot possibly have a complete grasp at present—that all assessments are *pro tem* and therefore subject to revision when we know more. This is certainly true of science, and if we are wise it should also be true of our philosophical and theological arguments.

CREDIBILITY OF DESIGN IN BIOLOGY

The theological/philosophical argument for design in nature is very old; it can be found in the Old Testament and in Greek thought. Psalm 94:9 is typical: "He that planted the ear, shall he not hear? He that formed the eye, shall he not see?" Of course, this statement is rhetorical—a warning that God is aware of the thoughts and intents of the human heart. It is not concerned with the scientific origins of our sense organs. Nevertheless, the rhetorical argument is based on the *implicit* claim that human hearing and sight are deliberately intended by God as means for a perception of reality parallel to God's. If we look with modern scientific understanding at the complexity of eye and ear as organs of perception, it is easy to interpret the claim of God's specific design quite literally. After all, that is the common sense meaning of the text—almost invariably a sound approach to reading the scriptures. Furthermore, the argument is not ended if we give a scientific analysis of physical mechanisms, chemical processes and organizational details. While these are important credentials for participating in the discussion, they do not sufficiently account for the *existence* of the thing (rather than showing merely the *efficient* cause, *i.e. how it works*); and most ID advocates make that philosophical point (originally made by Aristotle) in their arguments. Nor are the scientific narratives very satisfactory when examined critically. For instance, explanations offered for the eye's evolutionary origin as a "light-sensitive spot" originally performing some other function for the living creature (unrelated to optical principles), are at best imaginative scenarios poorly documented by real evidence. The *common sense* conclusion is that the thing was *designed* to be what it is.

That is why Christians should recognize that there is a legitimate place for such thinking—in *natural theology*. The claim that the God we believe in is the "creator of all things, visible and invisible" has real, substantive content and is substantially denied by those who do *not* believe. If an assertion of intentional design in living things is understood *as* natural theology, criticizing it is not scientific but *philosophical* argument. Furthermore, any critic attacking design in that context really assumes *metaphysical* or *philosophical naturalism* as an alternative to the doctrine of creation. While many persons in the scientific community do hold this world-view, it is not a theological option for Christians. In Chapter 2, I used the example of Robert Boyle to offer a different framework to justify naturalism *in science as a limited discourse*. Natural theology does not lie within the jurisdiction of scientific discourse—even though our thinking about it may sometimes affect how we think about science. The membrane separating natural theology and natural science should be defined as clearly as possible, even if it is not *impermeable*. The difference between my own view of the issues surrounding intelligent design and that held by many ID proponents is that these latter do not think the philosophical "membrane" should be there at all.

Because I argue that the legitimacy of *methodological naturalism* in science for Christians must ultimately be based (as it was for Boyle) on a wider, *theological* understanding of God's relation to creation, I also claim that our acceptance of the modern scientific tradition must be an *informed choice*. The almost overwhelming success of naturalism as a working presupposition of the physical sciences suggests it is a reasonable assumption, and no ID proponent has yet undertaken to "fix" the physical sciences by ridding them of that assumption. We must always be aware of the deeper theological foundation for our thinking about science. Nevertheless, making such a theologically and historically informed choice, I argue:

Intelligent design is not a legitimate scientific hypothesis, because it rejects methodological naturalism.

Almost everyone educated in science is familiar with the case of William Paley, who attempted to apply the argument from design as an explanatory paradigm for biology and even geology near the end of the eighteenth century. A thorough historical account of biological evolution *or* scientific methodology must necessarily provide a serious critique of Paley's "natural theology," which certainly proved barren and even obstructive for biology.[2] We need not do it here.

Similar limits of scope rule out any discussion here of the "anthropic principle" or the many people who have written about it. It is true that the constraints on the physical universe have to be "finely tuned" in order for us to be here and be able to observe it. Whether that does or does not require naïve excursions into natural theology on the part of scientists, philosophers or theologians is unclear. I tend to agree with the critique on that subject offered by the late Catholic philosopher of science Ernan McMullin.[3]

Many arguments and publications of prominent ID advocates today suggest that they see the force of their arguments in a context more pertinent to natural theology (or to speculation in pop culture) than to science proper—even though they may not acknowledge this. A good example is a recent Internet article created by the Discovery Institute about Alfred Russel Wallace,[4] a British nineteenth-century naturalist and a contributor with Charles Darwin to early ideas about evolution. My point here is that what Wallace may have thought about biology in the second half of the nineteenth century is not likely to be of much importance for thinking about biological science today. Discussing his views on biology is therefore not scientific argument, but argument in natural theology and is really directed to contemporary non-scientific culture.

I should therefore emphasize that this survey is partly concerned with assessing the works cited as to whether they argue for intelligent design as a discussion in natural theology—or as a scientific hypothesis to be developed via a scientific program.

A VERY BRIEF SURVEY OF WORKS RELATED TO INTELLIGENT DESIGN

This section is not a complete catalogue of works or even of all significant works on ID. It does provide pointers to the best-known contributors. For more complete listings of works on ID, the reader should consult bibliographies in endnote references given here.

The earliest significant contribution to the literature of the intelligent design movement is the 1984 book by Thaxton, Bradley, and Olson.[5] The focus of their work is the specific topic of "chemical evolution," sometimes called "prebiotic evolution" or "abiogenesis." At issue is whether or not we can account for the appearance of even the earliest and simplest forms of life as a kind of spontaneous generation from a mix of plausibly complex chemicals earlier in the earth's history. This project was begun fairly confidently by a number of people in the first part of the twentieth century who believed it to be only a matter of time before we would be able to explain the origin of life and of the complex information in the DNA "code" needed to construct it. Speculative ideas were the main contribution from the project for the first quarter-century. In the 1950s, Stanley Miller's synthesis of some simple amino acids by repeated electric discharge in a flask containing ammonia and other inorganics led to enormous enthusiasm; amino acids are the monomeric units forming more complex structures in materials like DNA. Thaxton *et al* describe in some detail the speculations and near-myths that quickly followed: The notion of the "pre-biotic soup" in the oceans or pools (not widely supported by experimental evidence), speculations about reducing atmospheres needed to form and sustain chemicals essential to life (not definitely supported by available evidence about the past). They offer a helpful critique of the way in which investigators have set up experiments to yield results in accord with hypotheses, rather than in a manner reflecting known conditions in the past. They examine a number of thermodynamic and statistical issues that make random assembly of amino acids into functional polypeptide structures extremely improbable. As the authors state, while synthesis of amino acid units under actual past conditions on earth is only highly unlikely, the specifically-ordered arrangement of these units found in functional proteins/polypeptides is fantastically improbable. The authors conclude by examining a number of speculative models for forming even the most primitive cells; they summarize conclusions reached by numerous scientists that no plausible scenario exists. I have mentioned earlier the opinion of cosmologist Fred Hoyle that claims about the occurrence of chemical evolution on the earth are not credible; Thaxton *et al* cite Hoyle's and several others' judgments on that point to good effect. In concluding, they offer in a separate "Epilogue" their own view that creation by an intelligent being from outside the universe is at least a legitimate philosophical hypothesis. This nicely separates the arguments of Thaxton *et al* in *natural theology* (*for* intelligent design) from the preceding *scientific* discussions (*against* arguments for chemical evolution). Such separation is important in arguments *for* or *against* ID.

In the same period several works critical of Darwinism as an explanation of biological origins were published. Michael Denton's *Evolution: A Theory in Crisis*[6] is noteworthy since the author was not a creationist but a secular writer who found the theory unconvincing. His work influenced others to follow. The 1984 book by Michael Pitman[7] is in the same genre but less persuasive.

The next notable contribution to the subject was Phillip E. Johnson's 1991 book *Darwin on Trial.*[8] Johnson's scope was much broader; he presented a severely negative critique of all aspects of Darwinist theory, arguing that the hypothesis of evolution of complex biological species by descent with variation from more primitive earlier forms is not adequately justified by supporting evidence. Johnson asserts that the idea was adopted largely for philosophical and social reasons, *despite* the lack of evidence for it. Johnson's discussion is thorough and based on a reasonable mastery of the literature in the subject, and he develops each topic with a clear discussion of what is actually known from scientific evidence. Chapters on scientific questions cover natural selection as a mechanism (arguing that it really *explains* nothing about why large biological change occurs); the inadequacy of chance mutation as mechanism; the lack of support from the fossil record for Darwinist ideas (no significant transitional forms are found between major biological groups); the lack of evidence for evolution of vertebrate species from earlier invertebrate forms; dispute of the claim that molecular similarities between different organisms *confirm* Darwinist *theory* by reproducing the pattern of the "phylogenetic tree" (Johnson's point is not that the two constructions fail to agree, but rather that closeness of biological relationship among different species proves nothing conclusive about an adequate mechanism for change); finally, the failure of attempts to explain the origin of the first life forms ("chemical evolution," earlier discussed by Thaxton *et al*). Subsequent chapters discuss questions of scientific method and rules of evidence, then the social and cultural role of Darwinism as religion and as educational indoctrination. In a concluding chapter Johnson argues that Darwinist theory is not science, but *pseudoscience*—something adopted by the scientific establishment and the culture it influences as an alternative world-view to religious ones.

Johnson's *negative* critique of Darwinist theory as "explanation" for biological diversity and complexity is thorough and severe—and is persuasively based on his approach to the scientific evidence. At certain points in the book, he argues that design by an intelligent creator is an equally reasonable explanation—but is ruled out *a priori* by scientists on the ground that it is not *naturalistic*. (That *philosophical* argument is central to the main concerns of this work, so I do not discuss it here.)

Johnson's book stands out most clearly because of his treatment of Darwinism as cultural religious indoctrination. His outspoken and logical approach to the subject has encouraged other critical responses from others concerned with the inadequacy of cultural totems generated by taking the "scientific world view" as a substitute for a much deeper understanding of reality.

Some Christians in science have suggested that Johnson's approach to evidence derives more from his training and background in law and jurisprudence, and they argue that in science it is often fruitful to allow more speculative and hypothetical interpretations of "facts" than those legitimate in the practice of law.

All the same, I think Johnson's negative critique of Darwinism's adequacy as biological *science* is sound at many points and should not be discredited by such arguments. Those of us who broadly accept the theory of biological evolution should not ignore its many conjectural elements, its incompleteness, and its many unsolved problems. Above all we must understand that it plays a role in cultural indoctrination not justified by its scientific status.

Johnson's critique has been followed by works specifically proposing ID as an alternative explanation of biological origins and biological complexity. Among these the works of several authors should be cited as substantial contributions:

In his book *Intelligent Design: The Bridge Between Science and Theology*, William A. Dembski[9] argues on grounds of mathematical probability theory that the specified complexity of information in the "genetic code"—and the resulting diversity and complexity in the biological organisms resulting—cannot be accounted for apart from the ID hypothesis. Dembski's argument assumes that the competing hypothesis is neo-Darwinist theory, *i.e.* random mutation plus natural selection. However, Dembski's aims in the work are considerably more ambitious than this argument alone, which he has presented in several earlier works and essays not cited here. Most of the content of the book is philosophical; Dembski attacks the historical tradition of *methodological naturalism* in science as fundamentally in error, although the only substantial case he makes for ID is drawn from problems in biology. A significant objective of the book is a kind of intellectual apologetics, whose core is ultimately the claim that "fingerprinting God" as creator and designer of the world is something we can do using the mundane kinds of inquiry open to scientists. *The Design of Life*,[10] a more recent work by Dembski and Jonathan Wells, covers much of the same territory but also contains additional details and arguments. Contrary to Dembski's line of thinking, I would argue that such claims create serious theological problems, because they imply that human intelligence can discern divine agency in mundane cases—cases other than the specifically miraculous events of divine revelation. In effect that amounts to a claim by autonomous human reason to name or understand God[11]—just as we can "name" or comprehend the created order of which we are part.

Stephen C. Meyer's book *Fingerprint in the Cell*[12] examines the specific scientific problems associated with the origin of the "DNA code" in much greater depth than the books by Dembski (Ref. 9) or that by Dembski and Wells (Ref. 10). It provides a good introduction to the detailed history of scientific work on the problem of "chemical evolution" and the failure of workers in that field to reach any plausible explanation of the information in DNA or of the origins of the simplest living things. In some ways it is a valuable complementary work to those cited above, and it has an especially useful and complete bibliography at the end of the book. In 2002 Meyer and I jointly participated in a week-long seminar at Regent College on the subject of design vs. naturalism in relation to origins questions;[13] though we differed significantly in our views, dialogue was open, valuable and informative.

Michael J. Behe, Professor of Biochemistry at Lehigh University, has made particularly significant contributions to the ID literature. His claim that biological systems even at the molecular level are *irreducibly complex* is an important insight (although some critics have tried to "explain it away"). I shall argue in the closing chapter of this book that a mechanist and reductionist view of biology *is* inadequate; there is much more to biology than the physics and chemistry of biological systems, and *irreducible complexity* is an important logical signpost of that fact.

Behe's 1996 book *Darwin's Black Box*[14] argues that design is evident at every level in biosystems. Some examples he presents are the bacterial *flagellum* (discussed in Chapter 3), the complex and delicately balanced process by which blood clotting occurs after a cut (Chapter 4), and cell organization at the molecular level (Chapter 6). The general theme throughout the book is that biological systems at all levels are logically organized in the same way as are extremely complicated machines, so that they are able to achieve sophisticated functions. At the end of the book Behe argues that such sophistication cannot be achieved without intelligent design, and that the likelihood of it having emerged by chance as per the neo-Darwinist model is fantastically too small. *Darwin's Black Box* generated a storm of furious controversy, including a rather stuffy disavowal of his views about ID from biological sciences faculty members at Lehigh more committed to Darwinian theory. A number of articles by Behe arguing for ID have appeared since 1996.[15]

In 2007 Behe published a second significant work on the topic of ID entitled *The Edge of Evolution*.[16] While he affirms the hypothesis of descent from common ancestors as supported by reasonable scientific evidence, in this work he takes a different approach: To what extent can biological change be achieved by the supposed mechanisms of neo-Darwinist theory (natural selection + random mutation + time)? As one model for his study he takes the parasite that causes malaria, since human attempts to eradicate it with antimalarial drugs have affected its evolutionary history substantially. Such a study also has considerable practical value, since understanding how an organism like this parasite can change its genetic character is important for the future. It is beyond the scope of this chapter to explore the book's argument in any detail; in the end, Behe argues that the malaria parasite possesses capabilities to develop resistance to drugs that cannot plausibly be explained as the result of random mutation. Behe's book also develops other examples which, he argues, require ID as an explanation; an interesting discussion is given of how a cilium is repaired or rebuilt by a scheme closely resembling an orderly construction process with detailed structuring of different units in order of time and place (*cf.* Chapter 6 of this book).

The greatest value of Behe's contributions to the ID literature is that he brings his detailed knowledge as a research biochemist and biologist to a wide variety of instances and examples. Most other ID proponents have focused their attention almost entirely on the problem of specified complexity in the DNA genetic "code." I shall argue that the concept of "irreducible complexity" is important to understanding biology scientifically, even though I certainly do *not* use it to argue for ID.

MYTHS ABOUT ORIGINS AGAIN: SCIENCE AND NATURAL THEOLOGY

For contemporary secular culture Darwinism is far more than a scientific framework for thinking about biology. It really is like a myth about origins, since (a) people use it to refute or reject other accounts or explanations with similar goals and (b) understanding the scientific basis and use for the theory is irrelevant to such storytelling. Insofar as this is the most important cultural role of Darwinism as an idea, its effective refutation by counterexamples that demand more critical understanding is extremely important. Arguments for ID are very valuable in this context, provided they use valid scientific evidence to substantiate alternative accounts of the world. This is good natural theology at work.

Whether or not ID is a hypothesis capable of generating new scientific discoveries is another matter. In this connection, an article by Del Ratzsch, Professor of Philosophy at Calvin College is of interest.[17] Ratzsch argues that the practical and scientific implications predicated by the ID hypothesis are indistinguishable from those based on alternative hypotheses *not* invoking design. While I generally agree with Ratzsch's philosophical argument, I prefer a more pragmatic line of argument: If ID proponents believe that their hypothesis is scientific they should demonstrate that by generating significant new research programs based on it as a specific platform. To date none of the works cited here, or any *other* publication by ID proponents, has done so.[18] This tends to support my claim that intelligent design is really an argument in natural theology rather than in science.

In conclusion: I do have some sympathy with people who advocate intelligent design as a way of thinking about God's creation of living creatures. However, such sympathy is *critical* because I insist that as far as possible we must maintain a clear distinction between discourses in *natural theology* and discourses in science; to be legitimate, scientific discourses should be *methodologically naturalistic*. Obviously the boundary between the two domains is at least a semi-permeable membrane, since the way we think about the world as a whole will influence in unspecifiable ways the way we think about science. Many if not most ID proponents deny the relevance of maintaining any such distinction.

ARISTOTLE'S CONTINUING INFLUENCE ON CHRISTIAN THOUGHT ABOUT CREATION

Scientists often remark on the baneful influence of Aristotle's philosophy of nature in the history of science. This influence was mediated by the long tradition of medieval Christian thought and persists in much evangelical Christian thinking about science. For example, belief in the fixity of biological species comes to us definitively in Aristotle's doctrine of the *Forms*; only by imposing Aristotle's teaching on the Bible can one argue that the phrase "after its kind" in Genesis 1 must be given the same strict construction. One way of understanding the ID movement is to see it as part of a modern contextual framework for maintaining Aristotelian teaching about biology and rejecting any notion of significant evolutionary change.

However, the biblical creation account in Genesis 1 suggests (in God's blessing of the living creatures, for instance) his divine authorization to explore their potentiality and capability for change—a potentiality with huge consequence in biological evolution. In the New Testament, St. Paul links the divine blessing with God's generous intentions for the entire creation to be "set free" and obtain a "glorious liberty," each living thing according to its capacity (Romans 8:18-24*ff*).

In stark contrast to the biblical narrative, Aristotle's doctrine of the *forms* is rooted in the underlying philosophical belief that a specified if complex pattern controlling each destiny is the means by which *divine reason maintains order in a material world teeming with creatures otherwise capable of immense chaos.*

This reading of Aristotle was powerfully illustrated for me by argument in a brief course I taught some years back on biblical and scientific ideas about origins. My protagonist was a Chinese student who had originally come to Canada from the People's Republic to study for a graduate science degree, and who no doubt had met their criteria as a "safe" candidate for study abroad having been duly indoctrinated with the appropriate materialist beliefs. However, in the course of his studies this man had fallen in with the local Chinese Christian student fellowship and had become a Christian. As a result, his beliefs about biological evolution had changed from acceptance to complete and radical opposition. My suggestion that the biological creation might be capable of evolutionary change (however limited) presented an immense *theological* problem for him. In our final class this culminated in his positive declaration: "If living things are capable of evolutionary change, then God's sovereignty is ultimately at risk." He had learned something about a theology of creation, but it reflected Aristotle's teaching rather than the Bible's. Struggling for insight, I replied that of course the limited capacity for biological change might be perceived as a threat to divine sovereignty, but had he considered the *much greater threat to it posed whenever we humans talk to each other?* I'm glad to say he understood my point and the debate was resolved by deepened faith in the sovereignty of the living God.

In claims made by ID proponents about information and specified complexity in the genetic code *having been inserted by an intelligent designer of some kind*, we can still see this lingering influence of Aristotle's doctrines about the natural world on Christian thinking about creation.

GREGORY W. CARMER

Gregory W. Carmer has been serving at Gordon College since 1998 where he is Dean of Christian Life /Theologian in Residence. He holds an M.A. and Ph.D. in theology from Boston College. He lives in Beverly with his wife Laura and their three sons.

PHILOSOPHY OF SCIENCE

Walter Thorson expresses critical sympathy for the Intelligent Design movement. His sympathy lies in with the critique raised by ID theorists against Neo-Darwinism and the attention that such a critique brings to the incompleteness of our understanding of the origin of biological systems. His sympathy is *critical* because ID proponents, in seeking an explanation of origins, abandon methodological naturalism and thus move beyond the bound of empirical science. Both his sympathy and criticism, I believe, are well placed. Here I will offer some thoughts from the philosophy of science that I hope will sharpen these points of sympathy and critique.

Let me begin with a succinct statement of three of Dr. Thorson's major points. First is that science is a limited discourse and relies upon other extra-scientific assumptions, agreements, and commitments to give it shape and to justify its methods. A second is that a commitment to methodological naturalism ought not be abandoned in empirical science. A third is that, in its rejection of methodological naturalism, the Intelligent Design argument has moved from scientific discourse to that of natural theology—a perfectly legitimate discourse, but not one to be confused with science.

THEOLOGY, PHILOSOPHICAL CONJECTURES AND EMPIRICAL SCIENCE

The conversation between theology and science is often framed along the lines of dialogue: science *vs.* religion, or science *and* theology. Such bi-polar formulations are much too simple and, in part, are responsible for some of the mistakes made by those working in this field. To this conversation must be invited a partner that is too often overlooked: philosophy. All three of Dr. Thorson's major points named above belong properly, not to science, but to the philosophy of science. And the philosophy of science lies within a field of discourse that is adjacent to empirical science and exercises significant influence on the direction of scientific inquiry; failure to attend to its contributions can result in unnecessary confusion and missteps for both the defenders of Darwinism and its critics.

I would argue for is a robust acknowledgment by those in the origins/evolution conversation of the role played by philosophical discourse in mediating between empirical science and other discourses. In the territory between theology and the empirical sciences there lie activities that conduct intellectual traffic between the two (and while theology has our attention in this discussion, the same holds true for other non-empirical discourse as well). This traffic impacts both science and theology in at least four ways, two of which move towards the practice of empirical science, and two which move from empirical science towards other disciplines. Let me mention them briefly.

First, as already mentioned is the *philosophy of science* which situates the human activity of empirical science within a larger framework and that, as Thorson says in his treatment of Boyle, "sustain [science] and make it legitimate."[19] The second is the expression of *philosophical research programs* that, while not empirical in themselves, impact empirical science in several ways, including: Directing the direction of research, suggesting fruitful avenues to explore, weighing the significance of empirical findings and offering possible solutions to anomalies that arise. Third, and now moving from empirical science towards other disciplines, is *making clear the deliverances of science* about the realities of the natural world which must be countenanced by theology and other meaningful discourses (such as ethics, anthropology, psychology, and sociology) if they seek congruence with what we currently know to be true about the natural world. And fourth, the mediating arena of philosophy helps mature empirical research programs articulate *auxiliary hypotheses* which connect their findings with other bodies of knowledge, suggesting ways in which the heart of the research program may both illuminate and answer to other spheres of knowledge.

These four functions (the philosophy of science which frames the scientific enterprise and philosophical research programs that direct empirical investigations—both of which shape scientific practice—*and* the clear statement of scientific findings and the construction of auxiliary hypotheses linking empirical data to what we otherwise take to be true), while belonging to neither empirical science proper nor to theology, are all crucial to the scientific enterprise. The failure to differentiate this territory of discourse has lead to some major missteps on behalf of proponents of both evolutionary theory and intelligent design. I will say a few words about two of these activities, the neglect of which is responsible for generating considerable confusion in this controversy, especially in popular works.

First, the role played by auxiliary hypotheses in mediating between mature empirical research programs and other bodies of knowledge. How does a naturalistic account of the origin of life and the diversification of species relate to other fields of knowledge and realms of discourse—in particular, theology?

This is not clear in the work of popular defenders of Darwinian thought despite claims of natural selections expansive explanatory power. Daniel Dennett, for example, asserts that: "In a single stroke, the idea of evolution by natural selection unifies the realm of life, meaning, and purpose with the realm of space and time, cause and effect mechanism and physical law."[20] But how does natural selection unify "life, meaning and purpose" with "cause and effect mechanism and physical law"? Here we have a claim of unity without adequate explanation.

What seems more apparent is the dis-unity between natural explanation and purpose. This disjunction between empirical descriptions and explanations on the one hand and the questions of meaning, purpose and ethics on the other is obvious to other champions of natural selection. Richard Dawkins, for example argues that:

"As an academic scientist I am a passionate Darwinian, believing that natural selection is, if not the only driving force in evolution, certainly the only known force capable of producing the illusion of purpose that so strikes all who contemplate nature. But at the same time I support Darwinism as a scientist, I am a passionate anti-Darwinian when it comes to politics and how we should conduct our human affairs."[21]

Such a statement runs contrary to the human and scientific impulse to find coherence and consistency of meaning within our world and ourselves. On the one hand, Dennett claims coherence but fails to demonstrate it, and on the other Dawkins acknowledges the disjunction but offers no compelling connection between the discourses of explanation and purpose. Despite the efforts of some socio-biologists to account for human traits such as compassion, forgiveness, and altruism, there remains a tremendous gulf between the naturalistic explanations of the world and the ethical convictions that direct our thinking on issues that are most closely tied to the theory of natural selection: The beginning of life, the end of life, and reproduction.

The failure of proponents of natural section to articulate auxiliary hypotheses that make significant connections between natural explanations of the world and discourses about the meaning of life has led some to assume that methodological naturalism implies a hidden, or explicit commitment to ontological naturalism—the belief that not only is our scientific understanding limited to the natural world, but the conviction that the natural world is all that exists. This is understandable. Naturalistic accounts of the world, which exclude notions of purpose or direction, final causes if you will, render a picture of the world—as wonderful and as beautiful as we find it—as ultimately, a "purposeless, indifferent machine."[22] This has led some to argue that methodological naturalism is the equivalent of philosophical naturalism.[23]

How do we bridge the gulf between naturalistic methods, and non-naturalistic explanations, where "explanation" is more than description and includes those questions we typically include with explanation—the whither, wherefore, and why? For this, nuanced auxiliary hypotheses are needed, and in their absence, ID proponents will remain suspicious of the distinction between methodological and philosophical naturalism.

The second function which belongs to philosophical discourse and impacts scientific inquiry is that of philosophical research programs. There seems to be at play in the argument of both ID theorists and popular defenders of evolution a construal of science that fails to adequately distinguish between empirical and philosophical research programs. This distinction appears to be missing in Dr. Thorson's presentation, as well. The failure to make such a distinction has led proponents of the new Darwinian synthesis to argue as scientific fact elements that remain obstinately non-verifiable, and likewise has encouraged ID theorists to abandon methodological naturalism in empirical science in a bid to make space for philosophical elements.

Here is how it shows up within the Intelligent Design argument. If we set aside the cultural and political ambitions of the Intelligent Design movement, there remain three principle strategies within the ID argument. The first is to offer criticisms of evolutionary science, pointing out anomalies and inconsistencies in evolutionary thought. This project may be helpful in the advance of empirical science by drawing our attention to the limits of our current understanding. Secondly, there have been some serious efforts to articulate conditions that define empirical phenomenon in need of explanation: Behe's notion of irreducible complexity[24] and Dembski's definition of design[25] for example. Thirdly, there is an effort to account for the phenomenon described by the above terms (design and irreducible complexity). In this account there is an appeal to the action of an outside agent.

Of these three strategies, the last is an obvious bit of natural theology and does not belong to science. The first, that of identifying anomalies and inconsistencies with evolutionary thought, makes a legitimate contribution to science, but that contribution amounts to neither overthrowing the new evolutionary synthesis as a research program, nor does it establish a new research program in place of Neo-Darwinism. Anomalies and inconsistencies with the contemporary evolutionary thought may be incorporated as puzzles to be solve or ignored as uninteresting anomalies in an otherwise fruitful program; in either case, they do not amount to an unraveling of the standard theory. The second strategy, that of articulating conditions that define empirical phenomenon, in as much as they offer definitions based on empirical conditions, are appropriate to empirical science and are sound contributions as far as they go. They are subject to investigation by others, suggest directions into further research and, in principle, admit contradiction and falsification.

In the concepts of irreducible complexity and significant complexity, the ID movement has offered helpful descriptions of natural phenomena with definitions that allow empirical confirmation. However, their apparent empirical status is placed into question when defended by the use of *ad hoc* strategies in responding to anti-design observations such as dysteleology (the view that existence has no "final cause" from purposeful design), suboptimal efficiency, redundancy, and apparent maliciousness within biological organisms. Moreover, in their explanation of the origin of these phenomena they have posited a causal factor that completely eludes verification or falsification. This is not to say that they are necessarily theological, or that they are meaningless—just that when behaving in this way, they are function as elements of a pseudo-scientific, philosophical research program rather than empirical science. Failure to make this distinction has only harmed the movement. By differentiating between the empirical, the theological, and the pseudo-scientific philosophical elements of their project, the ID theorists would bring greater clarity to the contributions they seek to make to our understanding of the natural world and avoid compromising the integrity of empirical science.

But it should not be a surprise that design advocates attempt insert philosophical notions into empirical science, for their opponents on the evolution side of the conversation have been engaged in the same practice for a long time. The elements of common ancestry and descent with modification of the new evolutionary synthesis are indeed empirically descriptive. However, other major elements are not: Namely, that the generation of new species is caused by the combined efforts of random mutation and natural selection. These elements began as philosophical conjectures in Darwin's original articulation of evolutionary theory and have remained philosophical through the theory's own evolutionary history. They have been powerful in directing research—as good philosophical research programs should—and have proven fruitful in funding research into the empirically-descriptive findings of common ancestry and descent with modification, but their status as the causal mechanisms of speciation remains a philosophical conjecture.

It is interesting to note that Sir Karl Popper initially judged natural selection—conceived as survival of the fittest—as tautological, simply stating that what survives, survives—but then later revised his judgment, arguing that the logical structure of the theory could, indeed, be formulated to be falsifiable and subjected to empirical tests. But, as Popper himself argues, it is not the merely the logical structure of a theory that makes it scientific, it is rather how a theory behaves over time and whether it responds to anomalous findings in progressive ways that attests to its empirical status. It appears that, despite its exposure to testing, natural selection as the source of speciation evades verification and falsification.

Three major assumptions of natural selection—geometric population growth, competition within and among species, and the gradual accumulation of mutations resulting in the emergence of new species—all lack verification and are countered by studies which demonstrate other natural restrains on population sizes, the presence of cooperation in place of competition and evidence that "organisms are [not] moldable in any direction without restrain."[26] Robert Augros and George Stanciu have assembled studies and summarize the findings thus: "All Darwin's premises are defective: There is no unlimited population growth in natural populations, [little] competition between individuals, and no new species producible by selection for varietal differences."[27]

Likewise, the sudden appearance of a great diversity of life forms in the fossil record proceeded and followed by extended periods of pronounced stability, while not in itself an argument against common ancestry, does provide evidence against gradualism. While the identification of conditions, such as geographic isolation, that contribute to speciation aid our understanding, they do little to account for increase in organization towards function.

It is not these findings that get defendants of natural selection into trouble, but their response to anomalies that marks the theory as philosophical conjecture. *Ad hoc* moves such as "punctuated equilibrium"[28] or the notion that transition from one species to another happens within "geological instants" that are too short to be meaningfully placed across geological strata, effectively remove speciation from observation, verification and falsification. So, whereas common ancestry and descent with modification can be affirmed through genomics, random mutation and natural selection posited as the mechanism of increased function tend to resist verification and falsification. If natural selection is to avoid the claim of being tautological then it must forsake *ad hoc* strategies for avoiding falsification in this way.

Likewise, the claim of random mutation can either be stated as a positive assertion in which case statistical analysis must be forthcoming to establish that mutation is actually random given the field of all possible expressions, or it can be stated in the negative, something along the lines of: "At present we do not know what accounts for the range of mutations that occur given the field of possibilities." However, these two postures tend to be passed over for a simple statement of fact that random mutations, naturally selected, account for the appearance of the species (or in the view of some enthusiasts, all of life). Statistical probability, while popular with some ID theorists, tends to be avoided by defenders of evolution, even though it is essential if the claim of random mutation is to be empirical.

Both the ID movement and evolutionary theory make use of philosophical elements that often go unrecognized as such. The ability and willingness to distinguish between philosophical and empirical elements of a research program based not solely on logical structure, but also on the record of progressive or defensive moves the theory makes, and to fully appreciate the mediating role of philosophy between theology on the one hand and empirical science on the other, is essential for scientific progress in understanding complex, evolving biological systems.

There is in the succession of species an undeniable arch towards intelligence and, as Walter Thorson says, organization towards complexity. To be sure, that arch is not without dead ends, cul-de-sacs and regressions, but the pattern of increased function is traceable. How do we account for such progress towards intelligence and function? That is the question that of greatest concern, not whether one species can give rise to another through descent with modification, but what accounts for the apparent pattern of progress in the direction of intelligence and increased function. The Intelligent Design argument, leaning heavily on the concept of irreducible complexity, posits an external, transcendent (super-natural) agent as craftsman. Neo-Darwinian theory suggests that reproductive separation, genetic drift, random mutation and natural selection (in addition to a couple other factors) account fully, not only for speciation and environmental fit, but also for the trend towards increased function and intelligence. I agree with Thorson that by positing an extra-natural explanation, the Intelligent Design argument moves beyond the practice of empirical science. Likewise, however, in merely repeating the doctrines of reproductive separation, random mutation, and natural selection, Neo-Darwinian theory employs defensive and ad-hoc stratagems characteristic of degenerative science and dogmatic interpretative theories rather than as an empirical explanation. A line of inquiry that probes the probability limits of blind mutation in maintaining and increasing organization toward function, and investigates the influence of yet-to-be understood mechanisms affecting the direction of evolution could preserve the empirical nature of our exploration and possibly lead to a greater understand of biological life and its diversity. Epigenetics and the role they play in interacting with environmental factors holds promise for this direction of inquiry and may be the "dark matter" of biology.

Nothing I have written here, I believe, is new to Dr. Thorson, but in his own treatment, which makes clear distinctions between natural theology and natural science, there seems to be little appreciation for the usefulness of distinguishing between philosophical research programs and empirical research programs.

Like Walter Thorson, I, too, believe that we are entering a new day in evolutionary thought that may soon lead to a clearer understanding of the forces at work that account for the direction of increased complexity and function of biological organisms. My hope is bolstered by the knowledge that scientists like Dr. Thorson are working to push concepts like "organization towards function" in the direction of empirical testing rather than fleeing the opposite direction towards the supernatural. Such research, I believe, will lead to a greater appreciation for and gratitude towards the Great Creator whose generosity funds this marvelous universe and the life within it.

CHAPTER 6:

BIOLOGICAL COMPLEXITY AND BIOLOGICAL FUNCTION

And God said, Let the waters bring forth abundantly, moving creatures that have life, and birds that fly above the earth in the open firmament of the sky. *And God created great sea creatures, every living creature that moves, which the waters brought forth abundantly after their kind, and every kind of bird after its kind; and God saw that it was good. And God blessed them, saying,* Be fruitful, and multiply, and fill the waters of the seas, and let birds multiply in the earth. *And there was evening, and morning, the fifth day.*

And God said, Let the earth bring forth living creatures after their kinds: cattle, and creeping things, and beasts of the earth after their kind. *And God made the beasts of the earth after their kind, and cattle after their kind, and everything that creeps on the earth after its kind; and God saw that it was good.*

—Genesis 1:20-25

LOOKING BACK—AND LOOKING AHEAD

In preceding chapters I have expressed a "critical sympathy" with arguments for intelligent design, based on a single point of agreement with ID proponents: That biology is in some way "*different*" from the physical sciences, or, more accurately, that living things are in some way quite different from non-living things, at least when we look at higher levels. Of course, a great deal of discussion has been given to the microscopic/molecular level; people argue that it is not clear whether a primitive virus, for example, is anything but a very complex molecular system. But even though they are scientifically interesting, such technical questions are not the point here.

In this chapter I consider, how living things are different from the non-living world. The main direction of the argument is the emergence of purposive behavior, *i.e.teleological* behavior, in living creatures. This takes a new direction from what previous chapters have argued.

In Chapter 3 I argued that an important step in the scientific revolution was the rejection of Aristotle's philosophical doctrine of nature, as expressed in his idea of the *Forms*. This idea is completely inappropriate to physical science, and discrediting it was essential for real understanding of the physical world.

Chapter 4 described contemporary culture, especially its ignorance, and argued that evangelical subculture partakes in this, having its own versions of such ignorance—with a resulting loss of influence on thinking people.

In Chapter 5 I argued further that many people who argue for intelligent design really seek to return to Aristotle's teleological understanding of the natural order, and that in doing this they reflect a persistent subcultural bias of evangelical Christianity toward a medieval view of the world.

The tacit issue behind all discussions in this work is the general question of biological evolution. I consider evolution to be a historical fact, even though I am not entirely satisfied with the adequacy of current theories.

I also stressed at the end of Chapter 5 that I have some theological reasons for viewing biological evolution favorably as an approach to the living world, in contrast with views like intelligent design that derive from Aristotle's philosophy of nature. These have to do with God's generosity toward his creation, a theme set forward throughout scripture. In relation to *biology*, God's purpose to give liberty to his creation suggests an endowed innovative potential exists in living creatures themselves. Certainly, this means biological change is not determined by a divinely imposed destiny like the Aristotelian "forms."

However, it also means that living things are not fully comprehensible using a model that recognizes only "chance and necessity" as the agents of change. But contemporary evolutionary theory is biased toward denial of any innovative capacity in creatures themselves.[1] In current culture, all kinds of complex behaviors in living things, even social and linguistic behavior in human beings, are "explained" as a consequence of evolutionary mechanisms. But I think there's more to the subject than that.

I suggest that at some stage in the evolution of biological complexity and variety, there is an emergence of creaturely purpose. Complex living creatures have their own purposes, and their behavior is best understood as an expression of those purposes. This is consistent with a biblical view of creation. We've seen in earlier discussion that God had his own purposes in creation; but he generously gave to creation a liberty to develop and have purposes of its own. Therefore at some point in the "emergence" of higher and more complex biological life, we should expect to see the appearance of an embodied *teleological* nature in living creatures. Evolutionary theory does not *predict* such behavior as a *necessary* outcome, whether or not evolutionary arguments claim to "explain" it after the fact. Chapter 7 develops this subject further.

The potential *scientific* question is: At what stage in the "great chain of being" linking bacteria, beetles, higher animals and human beings can we identify the emergence of teleological characteristics and behavior? Or should we say instead that all such questions lie outside the scope of science?

Christians in the sciences are always concerned to ensure that their own work meets high scientific standards. It is therefore to be expected that existing biases in their scientific communities have some influence on their perspectives on such questions. This essentially social pressure is greater in biology than in the physical sciences.

The next section is about "biological complexity," a subject of much current argument. The scientific literature on this question is far too extensive and technical for non-scientists to tackle, so I have instead discussed some articles written with generally informed readers in mind. The discussion provides an introduction to more philosophical questions about "teleology." The most important of these questions are deferred to Chapter 7, but in this chapter we do raise some important issues regarding "biological function" as an aspect of biology that stands out from the physical sciences. I discuss later in the chapter this difference, which has to do with biological function. In that section I repeat arguments originally made by Michael Polanyi, who described biological systems as analogous organizationally to machines ("the logic of achievement"). Since I have also argued for Polanyi's view, relevant criticisms of this analogy have been made by respondents. Nevertheless, organization *resulting* in function is a reality found in all living things. Today the term "emergence" is commonly used to label this aspect of the living world.

I conclude this chapter with a summary of the main historical, philosophical and theological shortcomings of intelligent design in relation to science, and in particular to biology.

BIOLOGICAL COMPLEXITY AND INFORMATION

Intelligent design arguments are directed mainly at the origin of the highly specified and complex information in biological systems. Such complexity is found at all levels of biological organization (though information in RNA/DNA is a particular focus). The implicit negative critique of evolutionary theory in ID arguments is that one cannot explain the emergence of this complexity on the basis of standard evolutionary theory [natural selection, acting on *random* mutations as a cause of genetic innovation]. My "critical sympathy" with ID proponents is based on a limited measure of agreement with this judgment.

The claim that *random* mutations can account for genetic innovation is poorly understood by people who are not biologists, even by physical scientists like myself. What is meant by the claim that gene mutations are random? Any decision that a *positive* empirical proposition is valid must be made *contra* the "null hypothesis," *i.e.* the *negative* conclusion that statistical evidence for it based on a finite sample of observational data is a chance result.[2] This means that if we attribute some outcome—or set of complex outcomes—to chance or random events, we are asserting that no alternative "true cause" is known to us. Any such argument is therefore really *an admission of ignorance,* unless the specific context provides *positive* evidence supporting that view.[3] However, critical commentary and explanation on this point is provided by biological scientist David C. Lahti later in this work (see his response at the end of this chapter). Lahti clarifies the technical context in which "random mutation" is understood by *molecular biologists.* Such clarification helps to avoid unintended meanings in social, cultural or religious contexts far outside the intended scope, a point especially relevant to the intelligent design controversy.[4]

As almost everyone involved in debate about intelligent design understands, the philosophical scope of the debate goes beyond the origins of the "information" in RNA or DNA. "Information" is also embodied in other elements of biological systems, not fully specified by that in DNA or RNA. (Because I am not a biologist, I cannot adequately discuss scientific details on that point. In any case, it does not change the essential issues.)

In this section I briefly survey a number of articles bearing on biological complexity. Some of these appear in recent issues of *Perspectives on Science and Christian Faith* (PSCF), the *Journal of the American Scientific Affiliation*, and have a Christian context: The authors are aware of the ID controversy, and their discussions bear on whether or not intelligent agency is necessary to explain such complexity. ID proponent Michael Behe has used the bacterial *flagellum* as another instance of complexity (which he argues requires intelligent design), and articles cited here also offer a good account by several scientists of the *flagellum's* complexity, to give a balanced picture. Still other citations are to recent reviews or articles in the scientific literature itself and have less direct relevance to the controversy itself. My intent is only to give a general idea of the interesting questions that arise in biology and evolutionary theory. Citations are chosen as examples of *biological complexity*, and not primarily as evidence for or against "intelligent design." I have emphasized earlier that the philosophical and historical issues at stake in the debate about biological origins are much broader than such technical and scientific questions. Some of these are discussed later in this chapter. The most important questions are reserved for Chapter 7.

In a recent PSCF article, biologists Harry Cook and Hank D. Bestman[5] offer a helpful discussion of (a) the nature of the problem requiring understanding in biology, (b) ambiguities inherent in the term *complexity* as a descriptor, (c) comparisons with other usages of the term in different contexts, and (d) comments on philosophical/metaphysical assumptions implicit in its historical usage. They include a very useful list of about eighty citations of articles and books tackling the subject both in biology specifically and in more general contexts, some going back to early twentieth century work in biology. While they do not try to discourage use of the term "complexity," they introduce more helpful ideas (such as whether an explanation is reductionist or non-reductionist). They comment on Ernst Mayr's use of the term "emergence" and offer interpretation of its contextual meaning by examples but without giving it a general definition. In relation to the debate over ID, they offer no specific opinion but seem to agree that reflections on design properly belong to natural theology rather than science. They raise briefly a point developed much more fully by Isaac and others (see below) that the DNA "code" does not necessarily imply intelligence as its origin but is instead a physically prescriptive device used by biosystems to create specific types of structures and compounds essential to biological existence. Lastly, they frequently use the term "function" in various contexts, which in my opinion makes clearer what's unique to biology.

Three articles published in the December 2011 issue of *Perspectives on Science and Christian Faith* have pursued specific issues related to ID. In the first of these, Randy Isaac[6] first lays out categories of "information" in various contexts. He draws on a long professional background in the field. The largest, the *"thermodynamic,"* is the conceived set of physical data that might be needed to specify all possible states of every elementary "particle" in the universe. However, this vast category is not a measure of useful "information" storage, and Isaac introduces a much smaller subset/category, the "*capacity*" of a specific system for conveying information. The clearest definition is: "The total set of all physical patterns that can be utilized for the embodiment of an idea is the *capacity* of information." He illustrates this with various examples, but observes that in the world of digital technology "*capacity*" is conveniently measured by the number of bits or binary digits available. Thus for a system with four distinguishable bits, each "0" or "1", the capacity equals 2, 4 or 16, while for 2-digit Arabic numerals, it is 100 (*0-99*).

Isaac's third information category is the "*syntax*": It is the *actual state of a specific system with given information capacity*. In the 4-bit system just described, it might be a particular sequence, like "*1011*." Finally, the fourth category is the *semantic,* in which "our usage of the term 'information' refers to the meaning or function of the syntax selected." Isaac illustrates each of these categories with helpful examples.

Of course, the most interesting category is the semantic, where meaning is linked to some sort of consequence. Formal *information theory* is only concerned with the first three descriptive categories—thermodynamic, capacity and syntax—and does not deal with semantic issues. Our most common experience of semantics arises from our ability to use abstract symbolism to impart conceptual meaning (as in language or mathematics). Since using abstract symbolism *is* a characteristic mark of intelligence, it is easy to jump to the conclusion that all semantic information requires intelligence as its origin; *and this is the inference drawn by ID proponents.* A key point in Isaac's paper is that (a) in the "DNA code" and other biologically active information, the semantic information is *not* abstract symbolic information; its specificity is *purely physical.* A given "code" sequence translates via physical mechanisms into making particular proteins; it has no abstract symbolic meaning (aside from our assignment of such meaning to it). A second point is empirical: (b) contrary to claims by some ID proponents, *new* "complex specified information (CSI)" of the sort found in DNA is generated in biochemical systems *without* intelligent agency. Isaac also makes several other helpful observations: (c) evidence from studies of genomic sequences suggests a common ancestry of all living things; and (d) mutations in the genomes (DNA) of living things occur mainly in those regions that are less critical for survival (a consequence of natural selection).

Isaac's conclusions largely agree with my own understanding about evolution: The great increase over time in both complexity and diversity of living things is *not* due to intelligent design; among the active principles suggested by the evidence are that (1) all living things have come into existence by descent from a common ancestor, (2) innovation is introduced through some process of mutation in the genome of a living creature according to rules we do not yet fully understand, and (3) natural selection by the environment acts to "winnow" such innovations for those changes that may improve the fitness of a creature for its habitat. Isaac and I likely differ over (4) whether or not these three active principles suffice to explain what has happened, and (5) whether or not "a combination of chance and necessity" is a good descriptor for a sufficient set of principles. I discuss aspects of these questions in closing sections of this chapter.

The two following articles in the same (December 2011) issue of *Perspectives* (PSCF) describe research seconding Isaac's arguments. Jonathan K. Watts,[7] a biochemist working on "oligonucleotides," shows in detail that new "specified information" can arise from *in vitro* chemical processes. ("in vitro" (literally, "in glass") means, in a non-living environment, as contrasted with *in vivo*, a living environment.) An *oligonucleotide* is "a short sequence of DNA, RNA, and/or chemically synthesized analogues" containing the fundamental "building block" nucleic acid/base units: Adenine (A), cytosine (C), guanine (G) and thymine (T); RNA also contains uracil (U). "SELEX" experiments by Watts and others in the field study processes in synthetic oligonucleotides that do not have the helical chain structure of DNA and have no biological activity. (It should be mentioned that such processes and the complex structures resulting are dominated by "stereochemical" properties, *i.e.* short-range "size and shape" features. There is no evidence for long-range coordinating forces in biologically active molecules—or in Watts' synthetic oligonucleotides.) Some ID proponents have claimed that the specified information in DNA/RNA is *conserved*. For example, W. A. Dembski states this claim as follows: "*Natural causes are incapable of generating CSI.* I call this the law of conservation of information, or LCI for short."[8] Watts' article shows this claim is incorrect: *New* information can be acquired even by non-living oligonucleotides.

Watts also emphasizes a second point made by Isaac: The semantic information in DNA does not have *abstract symbolic* meaning, but purely *physical* meaning. This subtle distinction is obscured by using popular terms like "the DNA *code*." If a particular information syntax is understood as a *symbol* standing for or representing something *physically unrelated* to the symbol itself, such information has *abstract symbolic* content and intelligent agency is involved. But Watts shows that in both DNA/ RNA and biologically inactive oligonucleotides, there is a direct physical connection between a particular nucleotide sequence and a resulting chemical synthesis resulting. Nothing in the sequence "stands for" things *not physically related* to it, *i.e.* there's no "ghost in the machine."

The third article in the set is by Stephen Freeland,[9] a biologist with background in zoology, genetics, and biological computation. He is currently project manager for NASA's Astrobiological Institute research team and is therefore appropriately interested in life's origins from prebiotic materials.

Freeland's article begins by discussing *methodological naturalism* as a presupposition of science, since this policy is challenged by many ID proponents. This is followed by a preliminary definition of the logical status of propositions concerning reality.[10] Freeland states: "Intelligent design theory has . . . started its life in Category 2 by suggesting that current evolutionary theory cannot adequately explain the origin of new genetic information. The . . . definition of evolution written above hints why many scientists, including Christians such as myself, think this is an incorrect . . . proposition." This statement implies that neo-Darwinism is/may become an adequate account of biological origins, and is similar to Isaac's remark that "chance and necessity" are enough.

Freeland's article also provides helpful information about the history of earlier ideas on biological origins (*e.g.,* those of Francis Crick) and relation to current work. He cites Watts' companion article and emphasizes the fact that sequences of RNA can "exhibit protein-like behavior" by folding up into complex 3-D structures that act like proteins (rather than the helical structure characteristic of DNA). This leads to a discussion of the "RNA world" as a plausible scenario for the earliest life forms and some evidence for it in the fact that RNA has catalytic activity as proteins do (as contrasted, say, with information storage, for which DNA is better suited). Thus RNA could plausibly have performed both jobs later specialized separately in proteins and in DNA. Freeland also mentions some difficulties with the RNA-world as a model for "what came first." He discusses earlier ideas that minerals (possibly in hydrothermal vents in the deep ocean) may have acted as the original substrates for generating complex information of the sort RNA embodies, even mentioning much older work by Cairns-Smith on complex *ordered* structures in certain clays.[11] Such wide-ranging speculations should be carefully distinguished from supported arguments.

Freeman's article further supports Isaac's arguments that the rich complexity of "molecular information" in biosystems can arise without requiring intelligent design as its explanation, and offers further evidence against the ID hypothesis.

All three of these articles discuss biological origins entirely in the context of physical/chemical phenomena. The authors' arguments, therefore, disagree with the view of ID proponents who argue against methodological naturalism in biology.

Biological complexity is also illustrated nicely by an example discussed in Michael Behe's book *The Edge of Evolution* (see citation in Ref. 16). This is the bacterial *flagellum*, described in Behe's Appendix C.[12] The most recent detailed account in the scientific literature cited by Behe is by Minamino and Namba[13] (2004); citations to other recent review articles are included, especially a 2000 *Physics Today* article on the flagellum "motor" (in *E. Coli*) by biophysicist Howard Berg. Figure 1 is taken from Berg's article. Figure 1a shows a rotationally-averaged electron micrograph of the apparatus, made by Professor David DeRosier of Brandeis University; Figure 1b is a schematic diagram showing its components more clearly. Berg's review article states that it is a molecular-size "electric motor," and describes proton transfer processes actuating it.

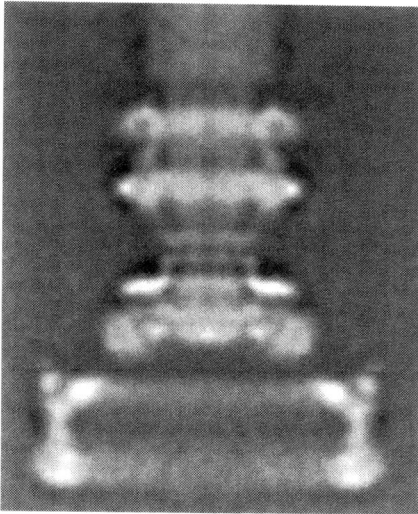

Figure 1a

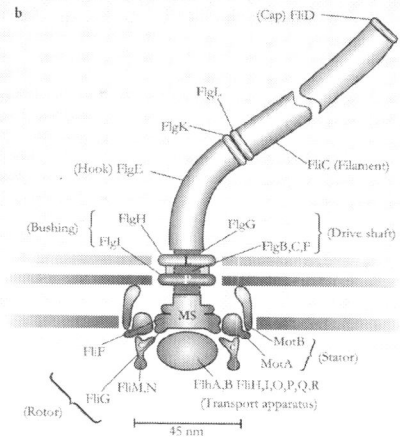

Figure 1b

Another striking example (one particularly interesting to me as a physical scientist) is the complex molecular system that converts light into chemical energy in certain photosynthetic bacteria. A brief account by Klaus Schulten and colleague Xiche Hu appears in a 1997 article in *Physics Today*.[14] One diagram from this article is shown in Figure 2. Readers should not try to understand the diagram, merely note the system's complex arrangement. The discussion given by Schulten and Hu is challenging and technical for scientists outside the field and even more so for non-scientists. I find it interesting because physical and chemical mechanisms used to achieve the photosynthesis function are worked out in considerable detail. As in plant photosynthesis using chlorophyll, the system is so arranged that *two* photons in the visible region of the spectrum are collected, following which the device is "triggered" and the combined energy of both light quanta is transferred to another site performing the chemical synthesis. (A single photon with enough energy for this synthesis is rarely available in sunlight reaching the ground.) Hu and Schulten are not concerned with the philosophical issues discussed here. However, their assumptions about *functional* organization of the system are evident to any thoughtful reader of their article.

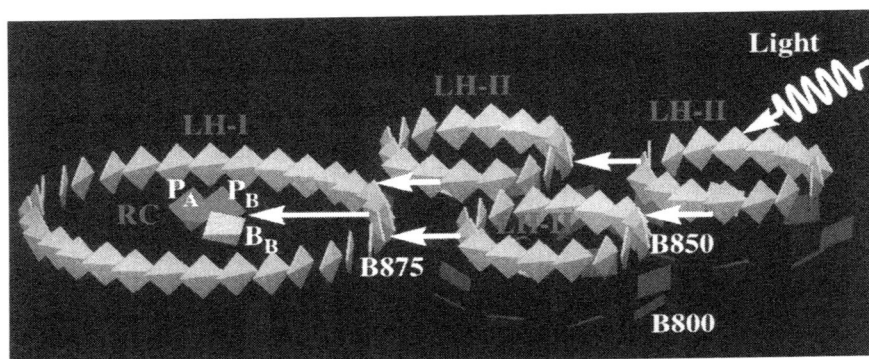

Figure 2

Many other examples of biological complexity exist. Those cited above give some idea of what such complexity is like. In the next sections I turn to the question of how biological systems differ from "purely physical" systems.

WHAT'S DIFFERENT ABOUT BIOLOGICAL SYSTEMS

The Weather as a Complex but Purely Physical System

We encounter systems in the non-living world that are also extremely complex, and exhibit phenomena we seek to understand physically. The best and most interesting paradigm is the weather. Here is a complex, intricate system that exhibits recognizable, repeatable behavior; yet we have learned that its prediction from microscopic physical principles is impossible because we cannot acquire sufficiently precise specification to make such prediction (forecasting) reliable for more than a short time. Studying weather first introduced scientists to classical chaos in physical systems (it isn't clear how "quantum chaos" is related to that or even if the latter exists).

In the weather, we have complexity in detail that leads to definite, coherent large scale events we describe as rain, snow, wind, *etc.* (whose predictability is limited in scope). But (apart from joking) we never consider ascribing to such phenomena any discernible *function* or achievement; that is, we understand the weather scientifically as *a purely physical system*. It achieves no function, and accomplishes no task. I think the contrast with complex biological organization is obvious.

To the extent that scientific study of biological systems is understood to be a study purely of their physical and chemical behavior in specified contexts, the claim that biology is *not* different from physics and chemistry is defensible. If we take only that point of view toward such study, the distinction from the study of weather is less obvious. But even the briefest reading of scientific books and articles about biology shows that other concepts, unknown to physics or chemistry, form an essential aspect of biological discourse (this is neither an objection nor a commendation—only an observation). Furthermore, this discourse appears *teleological*; that is, it describes phenomena that we understand semantically using terms like *function* or *achievement*.

FUNCTION AS AN ESSENTIAL FEATURE OF BIOLOGY

Even a little acquaintance with research practice and terminology shows that the concept of function is indispensable in biology. Research program design is based on the tacit assumption that certain functional rules operate in biosystems; learning what these rules are is the real aim. Structural characteristics and chemical mechanisms are necessary background knowledge but merely provide an admission ticket to the enterprise. Research terminology routinely describes component molecular entities by names such as *receptor, messenger, trigger, sensor, label, motor, etc.,* not merely by mechanical terms such as *inhibitor* or *activator* common in chemical kinetics. Molecular components enabling biological functions are described by their roles in the overall function of a biosystem, and the words used are meaningful in that tacit context. Some biologists argue that such terminology is merely a convenient "shorthand" for behavior that does not in fact imply any real function when analyzed in detail. At best, this is semantically very confused language!

THE MACHINE ANALOGY

Following Michael Polanyi's argument, I suggest that the concept of a *machine* presents a good model for understanding biological function. There is a danger my argument may be misunderstood—as an argument *for* design. In our experience, machines always have *intelligent designers*; that argument lies at the heart of William Paley's "natural theology" which proved so obstructive to scientific progress in biology. I should therefore state very clearly that I have no interest whatever in making it! It would undercut my concern with *naturalistic* explanation of biological systems.

Michael Polanyi was the first scientist to use the machine paradigm in the way I intend here: As a logical bridge toward understanding *how* "biology is different." The argument appears in Polanyi's pioneering work on epistemology, *Personal Knowledge,*[15] and has been understood by some biologists as an argument for "vitalism" in biology.

To understand any entity as a *machine*, Polanyi said, we must understand not only those physical principles on which it relies, but must also have a *logical conception of the achievement which its construction embodies:* That is, those particular *rules of proper function* which govern what it is and does as a machine. Without knowing these rules and their coherent logical relationships, one can neither understand a thing *as* a machine, nor fix it when it is broken. The indispensable character of this knowledge, and its *logical independence* of physics, can be shown by two simple observations:

[1] A broken machine, one that no longer functions properly, obeys physical laws as completely as a machine in perfect working order. This shows that there is a further organization of its particular mechanical parts required, that is *not* sufficiently prescribed by physical laws alone

[2] For a person who does not understand this independent *logic of proper function,* a machine, whether broken or not, cannot be understood *as* a machine; nor can it be repaired if it is broken. Instead it appears as a strange and meaningless jumble of physical connections.

Everyone realizes the truth of these common-sense principles when trying to understand (or *repair*) a complicated and unfamiliar machine.

The situation is further confused because, in the case of machines we humans build, the *logic of function* that governs the machine's proper arrangement, and the *specific logic of physical laws* employed in the machine's operation are isomorphic, *i.e.* have the same form (for reasons of economy). As a result we easily overlook the important logical distinction between two quite different levels of understanding, since *machine structure* and *machine function* are tacitly merged in our thinking about it as a machine.[16]

However, this logical distinction becomes relevant immediately if we entertain the hypothesis that some entity we humans did *not* create is in fact a machine, or appears to behave like a machine, because *it achieves coherent tasks or functions* (even if very limited ones). In such a case, our tacit faculties of judgment must be called into play and we begin to look at the entity, no longer as a meaningless jumble of components and mechanisms, but instead, in terms of some imaginative, synthetic reconstruction of the task (or tasks) it accomplishes, *i.e. what its function is.* Just such thinking happens in biological research.

I suggest that Lehigh biochemist Michael Behe's idea of *irreducible complexity*[17] has scientific meaning in this context. The issue is *not* complexity itself, but the fact that this complexity is essential to proper function of a biosystem. Without the particular arrangement of components present in the entity, or in the absence of one component, it is a "broken machine" and will not work. Where Behe uses this concept to argue for intelligent design in biology, I argue as Polanyi did, that examples he describes exemplify biological *organization toward function* as what distinguishes biology from the purely physical sciences.

GENE DUPLICATION AND BIOLOGICAL INNOVATION

Until the last two decades or so, we could say that while the evidence supporting evolution is generally solid, and also that natural selection plays an important part, little had been done to find out how innovative change happens in biological systems. Criticism of "chance mutation" as an argument without much substance seemed a plausible response. However, much recent work has focused attention on *gene duplication* as an important source of innovation. If a particular gene is copied in a strand of genetic material, something interesting often happens. One copy continues performing the function carried out by the original gene; but the second copy, while weakly retaining the same function, may undergo a sequence of "branching" changes that can lead to entirely new kinds of functions! This work is summarized in a readable 2003 review by Jianzhi Zhang (Dept. of Evolutionary Biology, University of Michigan).[18] Attempts to put some detailed meat on the bones of evolution are now making real progress. The process of gene duplication strongly suggests a biological organization with function as an eventual outcome.

However, important criticisms of my ideas about "biological organization toward function" are given later in a previous and a following chapter written by respondents: Molecular biochemist Craig M. Story (see Chapter 3) and physical scientist Randy Isaac (at the end of this chapter). Story's critique focuses on my argument about "biological organization *toward* function;" it is therefore also a critique of Polanyi's argument about the "logic of achievement" from which it is taken. Story points out that today we have a far more detailed molecular understanding of how complex functional things (such as the bacterial flagellum, etc.) develop by random mutation and natural selection. In particular there is no evidence at a molecular level of any "feedback loop" influencing future change.

Nobody questions that "functional organization" is real, *i.e.* that the biological devices resulting from genetic innovation do accomplish things as an end result; the issue is the implicit *teleology* in my use of the word *toward*. Story's critique also acknowledges that biologists' use of functional terminology in describing complex biological devices is semantically imprecise. While biologists themselves understand that no teleology is evident in the molecular processes occurring in such devices, they continue to use functional terminology (instead of more precise technical language) mainly for reasons of economy in communication. This can be and is misleading to people who aren't biologists.

In Chapter 6, Randy Isaac makes a broader critique of the embedded *teleology* suggested in my arguments. From a philosophical viewpoint, an important question about science and Christian theology is at stake. How should those of us who are Christians and believe in God as creator of all things look at the relationship between scientific knowledge about creation, and our confessed understanding of it as the "handiwork of God"? Like most thoughtful Christians, Isaac and I prefer an approach that makes them mutually coherent, with possible implications *from* each, *for* each, in the long run. Of course this preference runs greater risk of being outdated by discovery. There are philosophical reasons for it, and I address these in Chapter 7.

CONCLUSIONS PARTICULARLY RELATED TO INTELLIGENT DESIGN

The Plausibility of Design

In concluding this critique of the contemporary intelligent design movement, I would remind readers that the impression of design in biology is remarkably persistent and enduring. Denis Lamoureux[19] describes in considerable detail how equivocal and uncertain even Charles Darwin was on the implications of biological evolution for his ideas about God as creator. Arguing for the legitimacy of ID as a distinct discourse in *natural theology* offers one way of separating these strands of thinking about creation, though this approach also has its philosophical difficulties. In the long run, I take the divine blessing in Genesis 1:20-23 as a fundamental way to appreciate biological evolution's meaning. All living creatures have a potentiality for development on their own; in blessing them, God is granting them liberty to do just that. This is very far from the restriction of creaturely liberty implicit in the ID hypothesis. But it is equally far from the idea that our existence as human persons is a mere epiphenomenon of biological evolution

Intelligent Design and the Limits of Rational Human Inquiry

I have argued in this book that the "explanation" of biology offered by intelligent design short-circuits legitimate, naturalistic inquiry in science. Chapter 3 showed that Robert Boyle decided on methodological naturalism as a policy in science because he believed in the transcendence of a sovereign Creator, but very little was said there about the deeper theological reasons implicit in the doctrine of transcendence. It is perhaps appropriate to state these more explicitly in concluding this work.

The ID argument that "God's fingerprints" are detectable in the biological creation through mundane scientific inquiry is both theologically presumptuous and theologically naïve. In a 1957 book entitled *Mystery and Philosophy*, Michael B. Foster[20] writes about the notion of *mystery* in human experience. He argues that while modern culture seeks to remove mystery from human experience through analytic philosophy, scientific enterprise, ethical and moral philosophy, psychology, and even philosophy of religious experience, these human inquiries are all predicated on the powers of human reason; but there are fundamental mysteries beyond the reach of them all. What lies beyond the powers of all these analytic tools of modern thought is "the mystery hidden in God who created all things." In the chapter "Science and Mystery," Foster argues powerfully that what lies outside the grasp of science is that which is "beyond man's power to command"—namely God, and those things which are God's—realities such as peace, grace and love. If Foster's argument on this point is sound (as I think it is), then any claim to discern divine agency in nature by mundane scientific inquiry implies a denial of the biblical claim that the hidden things of God's relationship to creation can be known only through God's free decision to reveal them. The hypothesis of intelligent design is theologically presumptuous, because it claims we can remove such mystery using human rational powers.

In a parallel work entitled "Faith and Speculation," Austin Farrer[21] conducts an inquiry: Whether human reason has the power to discern divine agency in the world around us? The inquiry is presented in the format of a Socratic discussion, and one of the protagonists in the discussion is called "the scientist." Farrer's argument focuses on the epistemological problem involved; in particular, the goal of the inquiry is to determine by what means or kind of relationship to the object of interest any real knowledge of God is obtained. The essence of Farrer's conclusion is that the sorts of inquiry common to our knowledge of ourselves and the world we live in are epistemically and methodologically *inappropriate* to the knowledge of God, because God is not an object of human knowledge as created things are. God is that One whom we can know only through a personal relationship mediated by faith; the object of such faith is to know and obey God's will. If Farrer's argument is valid, the intelligent design hypothesis is theologically naïve, as well as theologically presumptuous.

Chapter 7 concludes my part of this book with a discussion of purposive behavior in animals, and its relation to philosophical concerns with truth and meaning in relation to the concept of "emergence."

RANDY ISAAC

Randy Isaac is a solid-state physics research scientist and executive director of the American Scientific Affiliation (ASA), where he has been a member since 1976 and a fellow since 1996. Isaac received his bachelor's degree from Wheaton College in Illinois and his doctrate in physics from the University of Illinois at Urbana-Champaign. He joined IBM to work at the Thomas J. Watson Research Center in 1977 and most recently served as the vice-president of systems technology and science for the company.

In these and related writings, Dr. Thorson has raised a most important question, which we might rephrase as "Does the organizational structure in biology lead us to infer that biology is more than physics and chemistry?" He has humbly suggested that perhaps the answer is yes, and that we might also infer that this "something more" has a characteristic of "teleology." I would like to respectfully offer an alternative answer, "no," on account of what is commonly called "emergence." In the next few minutes, I will attempt to explain, critique, and compare these two complex concepts, teleology and emergence, and provide a perspective on why I lean toward answering no to this provocative question.

Teleology has connotations of intention and purpose with an end goal. We might consider four different types of teleology:

First, there is the notion that the purpose and intent is vested in an external agent with some degree of intelligence. This is quintessentially William Paley (of the watchmaker analogy) and is the direction that the Intelligent Design community has taken in describing both chemical and biological evolution. Dr. Thorson has clearly stated that he does not support this direction. Much has been written elsewhere about why the ID perspective falls short on scientific, philosophical, and theological grounds and we need not pursue it further here.

A second alternative is that the system, itself, has some degree of intention and purpose and is to some extent capable of self-realization. This implies a measure of cognition or consciousness by the biological system in question. Again, this is not what Dr. Thorson means.

A third possibility for a teleological characteristic is the Aristotelian notion of "Forms" as Dr. Thorson mentioned in his lecture yesterday. In this view, there exist ideal forms to which systems aspire to achieve their destiny. Once more, Dr. Thorson has explicitly rejected this type of teleology.

Rather, he has taken a fourth perspective, which he describes as a "minimalist teleology." That is, there is an indication of intent and purpose in the logical structure toward function in biology but we do not know what it is; therefore the biological research program must seek to discover what it is and incorporate it into their understanding and explanation of biological systems.

The rationale that Dr. Thorson provides for his assertion rests on two main factors. One is an analogy to machines, following the path of Michael Polanyi. Essentially, the argument is that a machine cannot be constructed or repaired unless the intent and purpose of that system is understood. Similarly, he claims a biological system can achieve its function only if there exists, in some yet unidentified form, a purposeful intent or goal. In my opinion, the analogy between human-designed machines and a biological "machine" is too weak to justify such a conclusion. Secondly, he points to the teleological language that all too frequently creeps into the language of science, arguing that it is more than euphemistic but reflects a reality that we need to acknowledge. In my opinion, such teleological language only reflects the reality that we need familiar images and concepts to describe complex phenomena.

Now let us consider the alternative view of "emergence." Philosopher

Tim O'Connor from Indiana University defines it this way: "Emergent entities (properties or substances) 'arise' out of more fundamental entities and yet are 'novel' or 'irreducible' with respect to them." That is, the interaction of components gives rise to new entities and new processes that do not exist if those same components are considered independently in a non-interacting mode.

Like teleology there are several different perspectives of emergence. At one extreme, there are those who use emergence as support for philosophical naturalism or, going even further, for explaining the existence of the divine in terms of emergence from material components. We might think of Teilhard de Chardin and his view of evolution leading to the ultimate Omega Point that he identifies as Christ.[22] Others like Stuart Kauffmann in his book *Reinventing the Sacred* see emergence as indicative of underlying material constituting divinity.[23]

At the other extreme, we have the basic notions of emergence in the physical sciences, with which I do not believe there is any disagreement. Here there is recognition at each level of compositional hierarchy that new entities come into being from the interaction of the constituents. So elementary particle physics studies those particles like electrons, muons, and bosons that to our knowledge have no constituent parts. Particle physics considers protons and neutrons that exist due to the interaction of three quarks via gluons. Nuclear physics studies collections of tightly-interacting protons and neutrons; atomic physics combines nuclei with electrons; molecular physics connects multiple atoms; chemistry looks at the interaction of molecules, etc. At each stage, new substances and properties arise from the interaction of constituent parts but are not reducible to them. One might say that higher level substances have irreducible complexity or non-reductive physicality since they cease to exist if one of their constituent components is removed.

In between these extremes of emergence we have two fascinating arenas of discussion. One is the question of whether consciousness, intelligence, reasoning, and even the cornucopia of "love, joy, peace, etc." might be understood through emergence from underlying material components. Time is too short to address this question here and is therefore left as an exercise for the student. The other question of relevance today is whether biological systems are indeed accounted for by the underlying physics and chemistry, and whether the novelty of the organizational structure toward function is essentially an emergent property. Dr. Thorson thinks not, while I would suggest that it is.

How might we be able to resolve the question of teleology versus emergence for the appearance of this organizational structure toward function in biology? Perhaps we cannot. Neither teleology nor emergence is really a scientific explanation that lends itself to evidential support. They are philosophical frameworks that help guide the direction of our scientific endeavor. If either approach were to contribute to our understanding of biology in a way that is excluded by the other, then we might have a reason to choose. So far, it is my opinion that a teleological perspective has not yet led to the discovery of an explanation of biological systems while all discoveries to date are consistent with emergence.

But let me attempt to shed light on this question by rephrasing Dr. Thorson's original question in this way. Rather than asking "Does the organizational structure in biology lead us to infer that biology is more than physics and chemistry?" we could ask the question in this way: "What is the source of the information that determines the organizational structure in biology?" Perhaps by examining the flow of information, we can differentiate between teleology and emergence.

I would suggest that a key difference is that teleology implies such information exists in a static *a priori* sense, while emergence implies that the information is dynamic and *a posteriori*. What does that mean? A machine generally achieves a function that is specified by some design that exists independent of and prior to the construction and operation of the machine. There is an *a priori* blueprint which could be a detailed design drawing or an intuitive concept, but there is a guiding reference design, the pre-existing information, frozen in time—a static ideal. In contrast, in emergence the information arises as a consequence of the interaction of the components, making the successful information set evident afterward, rather than existing as an intentional prior concept. As we heard from Dr. Story yesterday, the primary, if not sole, physical function of any biological system is to self-replicate.[24] But there can be no prior blueprint of the information set needed for successful self-replication since the conditions for self-replication depend strongly on a dynamic system-environmental interaction that occurs later in time and is spatially separated from the process that forms the biological system.

For example, take a simple single-cell organism. To successfully self-replicate, it must be formed with the correct information (i.e., the DNA sequence as well as the epigenetic factors and the shape of biomolecules). But that information cannot be known with sufficient precision to serve as a blueprint, since at the time of the formation of the single cell, there is insufficient information available concerning the dynamically changing environment in which the cell will need to replicate at some time in the future. The flow of information follows the arrow of time, and there is no feedback to convey the "correct" set of information. Hence, no *a priori* blueprint can exist for such a cell and the teleological perspective is inadequate.

But how does emergence work? First, we must recognize that biological systems must be studied as populations and not as individual entities. Evolution works on populations and not on individuals. We must consider not just an individual single-cell organism, but an entire large population of such cells with sufficient variation to constitute a somewhat random spectrum of different information sets. With such a starting point, it is likely that a subset will emerge with the right characteristics for successful self-replication. This process is known as natural selection. The selected set is not known in an *a priori* sense, but is dynamically selected in an *a posteriori* sense. That means, it cannot be known in advance what the "correct" information is to achieve self-replication, but only in retrospect can we see which information set was "correct." For these reasons, I would suggest that the perspective of emergence is more relevant than that of teleology.

These are difficult concepts to grasp and there is much more for all of us to learn. I greatly appreciate the dialog Dr. Thorson has raised and the Christian spirit of his discourse. I look forward to a continuing discussion where we can all grow in our understanding of God's creation.

RESPONSE:

DAVID C. LAHTI

David C. Lahti is an Assistant Professor of Biology and the Undergraduate Research Coordinator at Queens College, City University of New York, where he runs a Behavior and Evolution laboratory focusing mainly on learned behavior in birds and humans. He received a B.S. in biology and history from Gordon College and a Ph.D. in moral philosophy and the philosophy of biology at the Whitefield Institute, Oxford, for a study of the contributions science can and cannot make to an understanding of the foundations of morality. He then received a Ph.D. in ecology and evolutionary biology at the University of Michigan for a study of rapid evolution in an introduced bird. Professor Lahti has been a Darwin Fellow at the University of Massachusetts and a Kirschstein NRSA Research Fellow with the U.S. National Institute of Health, where he studied the development and evolution of bird song. His current research projects involve co-evolution between avian brood parasites and their hosts in Africa, the genetic and cultural divergence of the house finch, the diversification of moral beliefs among African peoples, and the evolution of our capacity for morality and religion.

ON EXPLANATION IN EVOLUTIONARY BIOLOGY

I appreciate Dr. Thorson's careful thought about biological function, and the new and interesting way in which Dr. Isaac has responded to those ideas. I hope to take this track a bit further, and talk mainly of two things: Kinds of explanation in biology (this has been raised in previous chapters but not yet described explicitly), and what is left when evolution has had its way with teleology, or goal-directedness, in nature.

When explaining the traits of an organism, we can recognize multiple discrete levels of analysis or kinds of explanation. Respecting this point can avert countless futile arguments and misunderstandings. The evolutionary biologist Julian Huxley, in addressing the explanation of animal behavior in particular, saw three levels. I would say that they are equally relevant to all of biology, to any feature of any organism, not just behavior. The first is *physiology*, or mechanical causation, the actions of the vast array of bodily structures, including DNA, organelles, cytoskeleton, neurotransmitters, hormones, nerves, muscles, and so on. The second is *function*, or adaptation, the results of the action of natural selection on the traits of organisms across generations, due to the way environments influence organisms' likelihood of surviving and reproducing. The third is *phylogeny*, or evolutionary history, the patterns of traits that we see over evolutionary time within and between lineages. A fourth level was added by the Dutch ethologist Niklaus Tinbergen: *Ontogeny*, or development, the changes that an organism undergoes through its lifetime. Together these have been called the four questions or four pillars of ethology (the study of behavior), but today we should consider these more broadly as the ways in which biology can address the question of "why" for absolutely any trait, anything an organism does or is.

There is a nice symmetry among these kinds of explanation. Two are proximate, meaning that the relevant causes are within the same organism as their effects (physiology and ontogeny), and two are ultimate, the relevant causes being external to the organism and acting across generations (function and phylogeny). And, cutting across that distinction, two are mechanistic or process oriented (physiology and function), and two are temporal or pattern oriented (phylogeny and ontogeny). Not surprisingly, these four perspectives correspond to subfields within contemporary biology. My main point here is that the approaches are distinct but complementary. Each approach must be taken for a complete biological understanding of any trait. One cannot discover features at any one level by studying another. The same phenomena are being looked at, but with different glasses on, so to speak.

An example might help illustrate their complementarity. If we were to seek a biological explanation for why a particular man threw a rock, for instance, we would pursue one of four kinds of answers. From the perspective of physiology the answer has to do with, among other things, the brain sending messages over neurons to contract muscles, and so on. Functionally speaking, we might find that there was a hungry carnivorous animal running after him, and we might connect his behavior to adaptations that enable humans to recognize and instantly respond to immediate physical threats. Phylogenetically, we might start by noticing that throwing behavior is also present in our closest relative, the chimpanzee, and so we likely inherited that basic trait from a common ancestor at least six million years ago, if not far earlier; some squirrels can throw dirt at snakes, but they would have evolved that ability independently from our ancestors because many intervening organisms do not throw. And so that science would proceed. Lastly, a study of ontogeny would analyze how the ability and tendency to throw, including appropriateness and accuracy, develop throughout the early life of a human. Intensive and replicable methods are associated with each of these four kinds of biology. Here we have four complementary perspectives, all significantly explanatory, of a single trait, in this case a single event.

If we are to look at ourselves and our traits in an even broader context, leaving aside whether the perspective is scientific or not, I would add an additional explanatory level: *agency*. In the purely biological perspectives above, nobody bothered to ask the man why he threw the rock! This is because the levels were developed for the study of animal behavior, and we cannot ask the animals. But, regardless of where you stand on freedom of will, we can surely study behavior at the level of individual decisions for reasons and motivations, and the values that underlie them, and we can come up with conclusions that are just as distinctive and interesting as those at any other level. The study of agency may be informed by other perspectives but will never be reduced to them for the same reasons that none of the other four perspectives will never be reduced to each other: Because the agency approach is looking at something different; its methods and subject matter are complementary but distinctive to those of the other sorts of explanation. None of the other perspectives get into the mind of an organism, as distinct from its brain, and study things according to the direct experience, the beliefs and desires, of an organism. The reason why biologists don't study agency directly is because we cannot do so, with our perspectives and tools. Psychologists can do it somewhat, by asking questions of their human subjects. Moral philosophers do it too, by trying to make sense of our beliefs and values. From this perspective we would answer the question of why a man threw the rock in terms of why he thinks he did it, why he wanted to do it, why he decided to do it.

Finally, many of us might want to step back as far back as we possibly can, to the most fundamental level of all, and approach human behavior through the lens of metaphysical or religious beliefs and values. Here we find another, complementary and yet distinct level at which we can approach traits and organisms—that of *ultimate purpose*. A major aspect of religion is the imbuing of, or a recognition of, a purpose and a destiny to creation, including humanity, the validity of which does not depend on any biological discoveries about our behavior, nor on our actual decisions and values. The Tao, for instance, is the Eastern idea of a Way that is the fabric of the universe, and of which we are a part regardless of whether we like or understand it. And from the Christian tradition, a line in the Westminster Catechism that I memorized as a child states that the "chief end of man" is "to glorify God and enjoy him forever." Any behavior or other trait could be analyzed in relation to that idea and the results would be distinct from analysis at any other level. Even if one disavows any religious belief or idea of a transcendent purpose to our lives, no one can deny that it is possible to analyze behavior from such a perspective. Surely this perspective is not scientific, although it shares some features with science such as the search for truth and the criterion of internal consistency. Nevertheless, theology, devotion, and meditation on metaphysical things constitute a longstanding and potentially internally coherent way to analyze human existence and behavior—in fact, a theological interpretation of human life has a more venerable history than any of the scientific levels of explanation. It is the level of explanation that addresses the deepest questions of existence.

I will assume that you in this crowd would like, or are at least are willing to grant for the sake of argument, this sixfold list of complementary but distinct kinds of explanation in the study of life, four of which are germane to biological science (physiology, function, phylogeny, ontogeny), the fifth likewise arguably dealing with a product of evolution but only indirectly accessible to science (agency), and the sixth dealing with something that is not even a product of evolution and will never be accessible to science (ultimate purpose). The main reason I provided this outline is to highlight the mistake of pitting explanations of different kinds against each other as if they were alternatives, and to show how evolutionary explanation (both functional and historical) can always be appropriate, even though it can be inconclusive at any given time, and is certainly never exhaustive.

Given this framework, where is teleology, or goal-directedness? At first glance it seems to be in all of the levels of explanation in some way or other. The only two strong kinds are not at issue today: Agency is our own goal-directedness, and ultimate purpose, for those who accept it, is God's. We can set those aside. What remains, and what Dr. Thorson has emphasized is important for us to explore and understand, is the seeming goal-directedness that is accessible to science, in the first four levels of explanation, and especially in *function*. We must look at this more closely. What is responsible for function, or the organization towards function, in biological systems? The root answer, meaning the answer either directly or indirectly, in every known case so far, is natural selection.[25] There is no other mechanism known to science (and at this level we are restricting ourselves to science!) that can produce functional integration, to refine the parts of a system in such a way that they better accomplish something of benefit to that system. Natural selection is goal-directed only in a potentially misleading sense. It tends to produce a phenotype that is advantageous in an organism's environment, and over the long term seems exquisitely designed for it; but this is not because some natural process somehow anticipated that environment! Nor is it naturalistically inexplicable. It is because the environment, itself, skews the persistence of variants over the generations towards the relatively advantageous ones, through the inexorable competition among variable organisms in any given environment. This cyclical process, with mutation as a generator of new variation, results in ever more precise functional fits of the traits of organisms to their environments. The goal-directedness in this amazing system is not inherent in the organisms themselves, or in the process of selection, so it does not merit the term "teleology". There is a sense in which organisms have teleology in a weak sense, but that is development or ontogeny, not function.[26] What we recognize in the organization of traits towards function is an even weaker sort of goal-directedness. The biologist Colin Pittendrigh introduced a term for it in 1958 called "teleonomy," and I think we ought to preserve that term.

A process is teleonomic when it proceeds in a biased or particular way, not because the process (or an entity undergoing it) has an inherent goal, but as a result of the regularities or laws that govern the operation of the system within which that process operates. So natural selection results in a change in the traits of a population of organisms in a specific way in a given environment, but that is because that environment filters the population every generation according to the relative functionality of the organisms' traits, and this process together with mutation causes the population to change in those specific ways. The environment that imposes selection and the variation within the population are acting in concert as a sort of conveyor belt, moving the average organism each generation in the direction of greater fitness. This cycle rigs the system to improve the fit of organisms to their environments, whatever they may be. This kind of process is teleonomy.

In this light I would say that our issues or troubles with organization towards function in natural systems are a result of two psychological tendencies that are very natural to humans, in fact probably ubiquitous. The first is the difficulty we have in internalizing and fully appreciating the novel discovery of evolution by natural selection—the astounding mechanism by which nature becomes a system rigged to generate organisms that work well, and ever better and better, in their accustomed surroundings. A hesitation to appreciate natural selection can arise simply from a vague disbelief that it could work or be truly as productive as it is. Second, the effects of natural selection are remarkably similar in a general way to the effects of our own design or agency; and this similarity causes us inevitably to compare selection and agency, and sometimes even confuse them. But we must resist this temptation, now that we understand the biological mechanism, and we must respect the distinct roles of intentional and other teleological explanations as opposed to ones having to do with biological function.

I conclude with a couple of quality control points.

First, some concerns have been raised throughout these writings about the conclusion that mutations are random—concerns such as how we can know such a thing, what distributions and statistical tests would be required to demonstrate it, and so on. I believe that we can lay those concerns aside. They are an understandable result of the multiple ways in which the term "random" can be used. When evolutionary biologists say mutations are random, they still recognize that there are distinct causes of mutations, and identifiable patterns and biases in mutation. Many of these features are known, and in specific cases of mutation, causes no doubt will continue to be identified. All that is meant by random mutation is random *with respect to selection*: The likelihood of particular mutations is not affected at all by the functionality of the trait changes produced downstream from those mutations. The diverse causes of mutations do not include any feedback from whatever those mutations do to the traits that make them better or worse. If we ever do discover such feedback (and it certainly is theoretically possible, and some believe it exists), we will have to admit that mutations can be directed (by the environment), rather than being random with respect to it. So far we have not made any such discovery, and mutation remains random in this sense.

Second, I will take this opportunity to head off a strategy that certainly neither Dr. Thorson nor Dr. Isaac has used here, yet is common in some circles and often hovers around popular discussions of evolutionary explanation. This is the claim that evolution (and especially natural selection acting on genetic variation) cannot possibly explain some functional trait. This has never been, in my experience, a cogent argument. I do not mean that we have not discovered traits for which natural selection has not provided a direct explanation. We have. My point is rather that in every case where someone claims that a functional trait cannot *possibly* have evolved by natural selection, this is never an empirical statement. There is no way to tell whether that statement is true; and in most specific cases where it has been used so far, it has already been shown to be false. Moreover, the impossibility assertion is never associated with a mechanistic alternative, but only the endorsement of an entirely different level of explanation, which is not to the point. Instead of a sober critique of evolutionary biology, I find such a claim to be an expression of (normal human) frustration at the limitation of our knowledge or imagination. In our science classes, we usually emphasize the *testing* part of the scientific process. This is certainly important, but the opposite end of the cycle of scientific praxis is hypothesis *generation*. This is a very difficult part of science, and one that becomes ever more difficult the more we know, because every plausible hypothesis has to explain all observations to date and be consistent with or supersede all current knowledge. I do not blame people, especially nonspecialists, for not being able to come up with hypotheses in any particular case, say, of a plausible evolutionary or selective history for a trait. But if we cannot come up with one, that constitutes an exciting opportunity—not to make negative pronouncements, but to continue to imagine, think, and explore. And we should remember the separateness of those levels of explanation. We gain nothing of deep moment, absolutely nothing, by failing to understand the function of a trait in biological terms.

CHAPTER 7:

THE WOODPECKER'S PURPOSE

EMERGENCE AND MEANING

Many *naturalists* (as compared with biochemists or microbiologists) would consider my arguments about biological organization resulting in function to be truisms obvious to any careful observer. Authors writing in this *genre* have given striking anecdotal illustrations of the ability even of insects to devise innovative solutions to circumstantial problems in their environment. We have long since abandoned the word *instinct* because we find it does not really explain anything. We are equally unwilling to grant "real intelligence" as the cause of such behavior; we do not think beetles have purposes as we do. Yet at times they seem to act purposefully in novel situations.

A careful look at the biological "chain of being" between ourselves and the most primitive life forms shows a development from elementary behavior related simply to survival, through more complex sorts of organisms capable of considerable flexibility (*e.g.*, bacteria with *flagellae*), on to clearly sentient creatures able to respond in ways that force us to admit they are in some degree *intelligent*. I am not trying to discuss here what makes *humans* unique, though that question is a subject of considerable careful research today by people who study intelligence in animals like chimpanzees or other primates.

What interests me is an essential *continuity* in development of *some* degree of purposeful (and eventually, intelligent) behavior in living things. I have argued that the *presence of functional organization* at all levels in biological systems is an early and crucial stage in this development. One may dispute whether or not simpler viruses exhibit such organization, but the bacterial flagellum certainly does. It functions in such a way as to propel the bacterium toward regions of its environment richer in those materials it feeds on. The fact that this organization endows the bacterium with greater fitness for survival does not say very much about possible implications for more complex living creatures. While the hypothesis of biological evolution provides a plausible framework to organize our scientific understanding of living things, it does not go very far toward explaining the direction of their development. Why should intelligence and purposive behavior result from evolution?

Today many scientists use the word "emergence" to label this puzzle, but I find it no more *explanatory* than "instinct" was in an earlier age. As I understand the term, "emergence" means that at higher levels of organization, properties or behaviors appear that don't exist at precursor levels. This is an important and useful observation, but it is still fundamentally a descriptive term.

But surely it is simple arrogance to argue from evolution (and the notion of emergence) that "humans are the chance result of a process that did not have them in mind."[1] Such a philosophical claim is far too general. There's much more that hasn't been thought about in any depth. I maintain, as Michael Polanyi and also others[2] have done before me, that there is much more to biology than the reductionist study of the physics and chemistry of biological systems. Biological organization *resulting* in function is real, and in the same sense that "the laws of physics" are real. Polanyi's arguments about a machine-like organization *toward* function were discussed in Chapter 6, and objections to such arguments were also cited in relation to lower organisms such as bacteria (*e.g.,* the bacterial flagellum or the photosynthetic apparatus in bacteria/plants).[3]

However, this only refocuses the issues at a higher level. Given that we ourselves are observers of the world we live in, and that we are self-aware beings, at what point do we acknowledge something *not* completely accounted for by "emergence"—and in what sense do we claim it is real?

Recent works on "emergence" take evolutionary arguments a great deal further—and correspondingly, make the question of "meaning" more pressing. Among these, Terrence W. Deacon's work *Incomplete Nature: How Mind Emerged from Matter*[4] is perhaps the most fully developed. Deacon correctly argues that any complete account of the world must necessarily offer an explanation of ourselves, our sentience (shared with most of the biological world), our intelligence (shared with some other creatures) and ultimately our self-awareness, including such things as feelings and emotions, as experienced *realities*. His exhaustive discussion aims to account for these higher order realities associated with "mind" as *emergent consequences* of biological evolution. The question is whether or not this "completes" an account of our world; the implication in the title of Deacon's book is that it might do so.[5]

THE WOODPECKER'S PURPOSE—A PERSONAL ANECDOTE

The issues at stake in attributing everything to "emergent evolution" are nicely illustrated by a story related to the title of this book.

On the front lawn of our home some years ago was a beautiful "weeping birch" tree that my wife and I prized. However, it happened that one year a species of small woodpecker called a *sapsucker* had fixated attention on this particular tree. Sapsuckers typically drill a series of closely spaced holes into the bark of a tree, entirely girdling the trunk as many as 5-10 times. Then they return to the holes to feed on the oozing sap and any insects trapped in it. If the process is continued long enough the tree will die. In this case, we were determined to protect the tree, and often came outside to frighten the bird away with noise and menacing actions. As a result, the bird soon became wary of us and would fly away, returning to assault the birch tree only after it decided we were unaware of its presence (who knows what birds "*think*"?). Eventually it learned to attack the tree only after dark, or at early dawn before we arose.

Early one morning, just as we were waking, my wife heard the sapsucker at work and told me it was at the tree once again. Deciding this was the last straw, I grabbed and loaded a BB gun our son had left behind when he moved away, crept carefully around the house from the rear and lay down on the porch to take aim at the sapsucker, my wife watching everything from upstairs. (At the very moment I pulled the trigger, a neighbor was walking her dog right by the house. She had seen everything quite clearly but chose to ignore me and my peculiar behavior.) My aim was good, and I killed the sapsucker with a single shot and buried it later the same day.

The project was entirely successful. No other sapsucker ever came to attack the birch tree, either that year or later, suggesting that it was this *individual* bird that had fixated on this particular birch tree. The tree continued to flourish and develop further, eventually surviving at least 25-30 years.

At least two questions are suggested by the incident. First, did the sapsucker have some conscious purpose to attack this one particular tree? I find it hard to write the whole thing off by calling it "instinct" (or using some other descriptive catchword). Weeping birch trees are common in the area and the bird could easily have chosen to start over on another tree, since we had shown clear opposition to its actions. Second, did the sapsucker consciously understand that we intended to stop its predation on the tree? How else can we explain its very obvious change in "drilling hours"?

This incident prompts a more general question about the "emergence" of purpose and intelligence in higher animals. I am sure many other people have had similar remarkable experiences with all sorts of animals, including their own pets or livestock. We certainly cannot know what animals "think" or "decide", because we don't converse with them. Even our belief that other people think and decide as we do is based entirely on faith; after all, the only basis for it is that they speak and act as we do, and in doing so respond rationally to our own speech and actions.

My conclusion is that in some measure the sapsucker did "think" and "decide" certain things in a manner not too different from ourselves: The common sense answer is correct. But surely, if that is the case, then we must recognize that somewhere in the chain of evolutionary development, there appears in living things a genuine "teleological" nature. What they do is neither random nor meaningless, and to some extent it can be understood and shared by us humans.

It seems to me that this puts definite limitations on what we can offer as "scientific" explanation of their actions; in other words, "emergence" cannot truly "complete" our understanding of reality.

EMERGENCE AND THE QUESTION OF TRUTH

While Deacon's work finds a philosophical-scientific justification or rationalization in emergent evolution for our sense of personal existence as *authentic*, it does little or nothing to validate that sense as *true* in the sense that Christians use the term—nor does it address the further claims we make concerning *God* as ultimate truth. Deacon's arguments put us at liberty, for instance, to be existentialists like Sartre (see Ref. 8, Chapter 1) and like Sartre, even to discount the relevance of a scientific account of things to important aspects of our existence. But they say nothing whatever about whether truth claims, and especially Christian truth claims, are even *potentially* legitimate. For Christians and many others who share our view of the world, Deacon's work is still *incomplete* as an account of reality.

Since I am fairly sure Deacon did not mean to include such questions within the scope of his work, this is not necessarily a criticism of it. However, Christians (and many Jews) will certainly argue that much more remains to be said about such matters as truth, and other important statements we make about ourselves and the God we worship.

OUR INTEREST IN THE TRUTH ARISES FROM OUR BELIEF THAT WE ARE FREE

Concerning ourselves: Our interest in knowing the truth (at any level) *arises* from our understanding that we have the potential through our choices to change the future for ourselves and even the world we live in. I assume that like myself, most readers of this book are unwilling to abandon this belief for both theological and practical reasons. The practical reasons are exemplified in the scientific enterprise; the aim of research is to change the future through what we learn.

The theological reasons are less obvious but more profound: Through us as knowing agents, *truth has the capacity to shape the future.* Since Christians believe that truth is ultimately personal, this is a rational statement.

Concerning God, we assert, as Lesslie Newbigin[6] has so clearly argued, that religious truth is not a matter of personal preference; we firmly deny that it can be "true for us," yet not necessarily "true for all persons." I have argued in this work that "functional organization" in biology suggests that an element of creaturely *purpose* appears at a very early point in biology. My arguments may well be mistaken as to *when* it appears, a topic of considerable discussion here. Nevertheless, at some point in the "emergence" of intelligence and self-awareness that we consider essential to being a human person, Christians surely want to say more about truth than Terrence Deacon (for example) does! In that sense, while emergence offers some explanation of us as persons, it cannot complete the description of the reality we know and know in some deep sense *objectively,* since it is shared with others.

However, because I take the biblical view of history and the world we live in as framework for my philosophical thinking, I don't believe these modest claims about truth should be used to support unlimited speculations about human culture and destiny. Such matters are questions involving faith, not speculation. As St. Paul advises, we should think soberly, realistically—and not too highly—of ourselves.

CONCLUDING COMMENTS

This chapter concludes my contribution to this book. I have previously summarized (see Chapter 6) my main criticisms of intelligent design as an alternative explanation of biological complexity and organization, and readers only concerned with critical argument about ID should return there. I will repeat here only a general point: People who advocate intelligent design give up *far too soon and far too easily* on the potential of scientific inquiry to give an adequate explanation of living things, *using methodological naturalism as a presupposition.* They are looking for simple answers that short-circuit genuine understanding.

In this final chapter, I have raised questions that equally concern proponents of intelligent design—many of whom are fellow Christians interested in a sound Christian apologetics. In sympathy with those concerns, I have argued here that the notion of "emergence" is *unable* to "complete nature" merely by giving an account of human social and linguistic behavior (as Terrence Deacon claims). Evolutionary theory, including claims about "emergence," cannot answer our deepest questions about the meaning of human existence and says nothing substantive about truth,[7] something we humans cannot live without. People who are satisfied with this "completion of nature" as sufficient for life will exhibit that belief in their choices. A parallel and relevant critique of similar attempts to account for human personal behavior purely in terms of evolutionary theory was given in 2001 by theologian John F. Haught.[8]

Christian faith goes further than such negative criticism. This is because we are motivated to share genuine knowledge of God and God's truth with all who want to know him. When we make the Christian confession, beginning with "I believe in one God, the Father Almighty, Creator of all things visible and invisible . . ." and ending "and I expect the resurrection of the dead and the life of the world to come," we are asserting that someone/something *real and true* is knowable by all human beings, as well as already known to us who believe. However, I and my coauthors do *not* claim, as ID proponents do, that evidence for this reality is available mundanely, *i.e.* without personal commitment to God as a potential outcome.

END NOTES

CHAPTER 1: INTRODUCTION

1. See also Psalm 115:1-18 for a much fuller exposition of this point.
2. Although arguments for design go back much earlier than 1980, discussing them is outside the scope of this work.
3. Michael Polanyi, *Personal Knowledge: Towards a Post-Critical Philosophy*. Routledge and Kegan Paul, London and the University of Chicago Press, Chicago (1958); Second printing (with corrections) 1962. Currently available in paperback edition: (1974, University of Chicago Press, Chicago, IL 60637; ISBN 978-0226672885)

CHAPTER 2: FOUR CREATION PSALMS

1. Michael Polanyi has described the phenomenon of "integration" very clearly in his remarkable book on the epistemology of science: *cf.* Michael Polanyi, *Personal Knowledge: Towards a Post-Critical Philosophy*. Routledge and Kegan Paul, London, and University of Chicago Press, Chicago (1958); second printing (with corrections) 1962. Currently available in paperback edition (1974, University of Chicago Press, Chicago, IL 60637; ISBN 978-0226672885).
2. Today's world and its problems (*e.g.*, crime) often display these two ways of thinking, as media commentators seek solutions: Those who think action is imperative, and those who seek understanding before taking action.
3. Hebrews 2:5-18. The point of the exposition is to affirm the true humanity of Messiah, and the reasons for it. The author already has established the deity of Messiah and oneness with the Father in Chapter 1.
4. See for example *The Complete Poems of Emily Dickinson,* Thomas H. Johnson, Editor. (Hardcover edition 1960, Little, Brown and Company, Boston, MA; paperback ed. 1961; ISBN 0-316-18913-6). For this and other famous poems cited, reference is given first to a currently available volume by the original author; almost any anthology of English and American nineteenth and twentieth century poetry will also include it.
5. A deeper understanding of the biblical narrative about Cain and his descendants (Genesis 4:1-24) is given by Jacques Ellul: See Jacques Ellul, *The Meaning of the City* (Hardcover edition 1970, ASIN B0000CPIJ4; paperback ed. 1970, ISBN 978-0802815552, Wm. B. Eerdmans Publishing Co.,

Grand Rapids, MI 49505; reprinted with permission, 1993, Regent College Bookstore, Vancouver, BC, Canada V6T 2E4.

6. *Cf.* C. S. Lewis, the science fiction trilogy: (a) *Out of the Silent Planet* (1938, Bodley Head Ltd., London; paperback edition 1952, Pan Books Ltd., London; numerous later reprintings and editions). (b) *Voyage to Venus (Perelandra)* (1938, Bodley Head Ltd., London; paperback ed. 1952, Pan Books Ltd., London; numerous later reprintings and editions). (c) *That Hideous Strength* (1945, Bodley Head Ltd., London; paperback edition (abridged) 1955, Pan Books Ltd., London; numerous later reprintings and editions). See also: (d) C. S. Lewis, "Religion and Rocketry", essay published in *The World's Last Night* (1958: Harcourt Brace & Co., New York); (e) "Dogma and the Universe", essay published in *God in the Dock: Essays on Theology and Ethics* (Walter Hooper, Ed.) (1972: Wm. B. Eerdmans Publishing Company, Grand Rapids, MI).

7. See for example Karl Heim's commentary on "the enigma of personal existence", in *Christian Faith and Natural Science, Chapter II: The Ego and the World* (1949: *Der Christliche Gottesglaube und die Naturwissenchaft;* English translation, 1953, SCM Press LTD, London, UK (out of print). Heim's commentary seems to have been influenced by the controversial German existentialist philosopher Martin Heidegger's book "Being and Time"(M. Heidegger, *Sein und Zeit, 1927*; Eng. Translation 1962, J. Macquarrie and E. Robinson, reprinted 2008, Harper Perennial Modern Classics, HarperCollins Publishing, New York, NY 10022 , ISBN 978-0061575593).

8. Francis Thompson, *The Hound of Heaven.* Current paperback edition: Francis Thompson, *The Hound of Heaven and Other Poems* (2011, Branden Publishing Co., Wellesley, MA USA 02482, ISBN 978-0828314404)

9. Gerard Manley Hopkins, *God's Grandeur ('The world is charged with the grandeur of God')*: See *Gerard Manley Hopkins: Poems and Prose* (Penguin Classic Paperback Edition, W. H. Gardner 1953, 1963; reprinted 1985, Penguin Putnam Inc., New York, NY, USA 10014; ISBN 978-0140420159)

10. Jean Paul Sartre, *L'existentialism est un humanisme* Translation, *Existentialism is a Humanism*: (current paperback edition, 2007, Yale University Press, New Haven, CT 06511-8909; ISBN 978-0300115468)

11. Robert M. Pirsig, *Zen and the Art of Motorcycle Maintenance: An Inquiry into Values.* (orig. publ. 1974; paper-back ed. 2008, William Morrow Div. of HarperCollins Publishing, New York, NY, USA 10022; ISBN 978-0061673733)

12. Lynn White, "Continuing the Conversation", in *Western Man and the American Mind,* Ian Barbour, Ed., p. 63 (1973: Addison-Wesley Publishing Company, Reading, MA)

13. Loren Wilkinson, Ed., *EARTH KEEPING: Christian Stewardship of Natural Resources.* (1980: Wm B. Eerdmans Publishing Company, Grand Rapids, MI, USA 49505; ISBN 0-8028-1834-X; contributing authors are Fellows of the Calvin Center for Christian Scholarship, Calvin College.) Revised Edition, Loren Wilkinson, Peter de Vos, Calvin B. de Witt, *EARTHKEEP-*

ING IN THE NINETIES: Stewardship of Creation (1991: Wm. B. Eerdmans Publishing Company, Grand Rapids, MI 49505; ISBN 978-0802805348)

MARVIN R. WILSON RESPONSE

14. Abraham Joshua Heschel, *God in Search of Man,* (New York: Harper & Row, 1955), pages 43-99.

15. George Foot Moore, *Judaism in the First Centuries of the Christian Era* (Cambridge: Harvard University Press, 1927, 2:240; cf. 217ff).

CHAPTER 3: FOURTH DAY THINGS

1. Emmanuel Kant, whose concern with *epistemology* has dominated modern philosophy and intellectual history, reflects the same two-fold order in his famous work *The Critique of Pure Reason*: According to Kant, knowledge is an entity to which our reason contributes *form* and our experience *content*. We need not agree with him to recognize the importance of this binary structure for thinking.

2. Howard Van Till uses the fourth day of creation in a similar symbolic way: See H. Van Till, *The Fourth Day: What the Heavens are Telling us about Creation* (1986: Wm. B. Eerdmans Publishing Company, Grand Rapids, MI 49505; ISBN 978-0802801784)

3. See (a) Joseph Silk, *The Big Bang* (1986: W. H. Freeman & Co., New York, NY; paperback ed., ISBN 978-0716719977); (b) Frank Close, *The Cosmic Onion: Quarks and the Nature of the Universe* (1986: American Institute of Physics, College Park, MD, USA 20740-3843 & Melville, NY, USA 11747; paperback ed., ISBN 978-0883184912); and references cited in these two works.

4. See P. D. Nicholson, D. P. Hamilton, K. Mathews and C. F. Yoder, *"New Observations of Saturn's Co-orbital Satellites",* ICARUS 100, 464-484 (1992), and references cited therein.

5. This point about naming explains why, in the Old Testament, God never replies trivially to requests about his name from those who have met him personally, answering either with an identification based on what he shows himself to be in relationship to them; or more deeply, with a statement of his transcendence with respect to the world; the Hebrew YHWH, which the English OT renders as LORD, is the continuing assertion of this 'unnameable' character.

6. Feynman's books are nearly all wonderfully entertaining, but for scholarly appreciation I recommend two as examples: (a) R. P. Feynman, *The Character of Physical Law* (1967: MIT Press, Cambridge, MA, USA 02142-1493; ISBN 978-0262560030); R. P. Feynman, R. B. Leighton and M. Sands, *The Feynman Lectures on Physics* (3 Volume Set) (Paperback Ed. 1970, Addison Wesley Longman, Boston, MA 02116; ISBN 978-0201021158).

7. Of course such a boast must be qualified since it is fundamental to scien-

tific enterprise that its practitioners are always at risk of sudden surprise by contrary evidence. The recent claim (September 2011) that neutrino speeds exceed that of light challenges the well-established theory of relativity worked out by Einstein in this way.

8. Although chemistry has some dim empirical antecedents in medieval alchemy, its modern development in the tradition of Priestly, Lavoisier and Dalton more accurately places it in the framework of the mechanical philosophy.

9. This is evident in two unfortunate ideas whose influence we owe to Newton. (a) "God of the gaps" thinking: It was Newton who first made the suggestion that, where mechanics might prove incomplete or inadequate to explain observed behavior, instead from time to time God would intervene to adjust the system. (b) Newton's apparent inability to separate metaphysical speculations about divine agency in nature from his understanding of physical science led him to waste his considerable talents inquiring how God's activity might be discerned from experimental studies. Both notions have persisted historically and are implicit influences in the current controversy over intelligent design.

10. R. Hooykaas, *Religion and the Rise of Modern Science.* Originally published 1972, Scottish Academic Press, Ltd., Edinburgh; paperback ed. 1973. Reprinted in paperback 1980, Wm. B. Eerdmans Publ. Co., Grand Rapids MI. 49505; now out of print)

11. Eugene M. Klaaren, *Religious Origins of Modern Science.* (1977, Wm. B. Eerdmans Publ. Co., Grand Rapids MI 49505; ISBN 0-8020-1683-5) A second edition: *Religious Origins of Modern Science: Belief in Creation in Seventeenth Century Thought,* is available currently: (1986, Rowman and Littlefield, Lanham, MD 20706; ISBN 978-0819149220). See also more recent works by Steven Shapin: (1) *A Social History of Truth: Civility and Science in Seventeenth-Century England* (1994: University of Chicago Press, Chicago, IL 60637); (2) *Never Pure: Historical Studies of Science as if It was Produced by People with Bodies, Situated in Time, Space, Culture, and Society, and Struggling for Credibility and Authority* (2010: Johns Hopkins University Press, Baltimore, MD 21218)

12. I must emphasize here that I certainly do not deny the possibility of divine intervention in the natural order, *i.e.* the reality of miracles, since I have witnessed a few such events personally. What concerns me is the tendency of some believers to view even the mundane events of the natural world as evidence of God's complicity in them.

13. Alexander Pope, *Essay on Man.* See *Alexander Pope: The Major Works,* Pat Rogers, Ed. (Oxford World's Classics Series) (reissued 2009, Oxford University Press USA, New York, NY 10016; ISBN 978-0199537617). This famous poem can often be found in many anthologies of English poetry (17th and 18th centuries).

CHAPTER 4: CONTEMPORARY CULTURE—AND EVANGELICAL SUBCULTURE

1. For example, see David Blankenhorn, *Fatherless America: Confronting our most urgent social problem* (1995: Harper-Collins Publishers, New York, NY ISBN 0-465-01483-6; Paperback ed. 1996, ISBN 0-06-092683-X)

2. Several statistical surveys have been published by groups interested in the effect of religious faith on divorce. Not all of these agree on the details or causes, but divorce is common enough among professing evangelical Christians to be worth notice. See the 2008 survey by the Barna Group, www.barna.org/barna-update/article/15-familykids/42-new-marriage-and-divorce-statistics-released; also, more recent commentary on the same question, at http://usatoday30.usatoday.com/news/religion/2011-03-14-divorce-christians_N.htm. These two sources differ in their interpretations of the data, but people involved in counseling about marital problems all recognize the frequency of divorce is increasing rapidly, even in Christian families. I can also bear witness to the facts from personal experience counseling friends who have gone through a divorce.

3. Theological commentary on both Old and New Testaments has argued that God's purpose in the marriage relationship is to teach human beings the meaning of *agape*—the self-giving divine love that is not based merely on attraction or common interests, but is the dynamic of the Holy Trinity.

4. Some account of this history, and the rise of young-earth creationism as a reaction to ideas about biological evolution, is given by Ronald Numbers: See Ronald L. Numbers, *The Creationists: The Evolution of Scientific Creationism* (1992: University of California Press, Berkeley and Los Angeles, California, ISBN 0-520-08393-8). A brief account from a more secular perspective can also be found in Peter J. Bowler, *Evolution: The History of an Idea* (1984: University of California Press, Berkeley and Los Angeles, California, ISBN 0-520-04880-6; paperback edition, ISBN 0-520-04890-3). Bowler treats the subject carefully and fairly, though he concedes more to the adequacy of neo-Darwinist theory than I think justified.

5. Robert Jastrow, *God and the Astronomers* (1978: W. W. Norton & Co., New York; 2nd Printing, 1992: W. W. Norton & Co., New York, ISBN 0393850056; 2nd Ed., 2000: The Readers Library Publishing Co., Ltd., London, UK, ISBN 0393850064).

6. The best known of these is Hugh Ross, trained in physics and astronomy, who has used the evidence for the standard cosmological model as an apologetic for his interpretation of Genesis 1 and an argument against the absurdities of young-earth creationism as outmoded. See Hugh Ross, *The Fingerprint of God* (1989, 1991: Reasons to Believe: Promise Publishing Co., Orange, California 92667, ISBN 0-939497-18-2). Ross now pastors a church whose origins are linked to his views about Genesis 1, and has developed a wide following through his website and organization "Reasons to Believe," to which many of similar convictions contribute. Ross's views

on biology still mostly follow the traditional evangelical line of opposition to any concept of biological evolution, and the website endorses intelligent design as an alternative account of biological origins.

7. Carl Sagan, *Cosmos* (1985: Ballantine Books, Div. of Random House Publishing Group, New York, ISBN 0-345-3311354); *The Dragons of Eden: Speculations on the Evolution of Human Intelligence* (1986; Ballantine Books, Div. of Random House Publishing Group, New York, ISBN 0-345346297). Sagan's statements about science would be more reputable had he not (like some other authors cited in this chapter) also used them to argue that scientific knowledge makes belief in God superfluous.

8. Stephen W. Hawking, *A Brief History of Time* (original printing 1988; current edition 1998, Bantam Books, London, New York and elsewhere, ISBN 978-0553380163)

9. Theoretical speculation about other universes should be tempered by the fact that our own universe is the only one we know about and (as far as we know at present) there is no way we could ever obtain experimental evidence of others from within our own. There's no law against speculation, but it ought not to be marketed as truth. More balanced treatment of what physicists actually think they know about the standard cosmological model can be found in (a) Joseph Silk, *The Big Bang* (1980; rev. ed., 1989, W. H. Freeman & Co., New York, ISBN 0-7167-1812-X; (b) Frank Close, *The Cosmic Onion* (1983; reprinted 1984, 1985, 1986, Heinemann Educational Books Ltd., under auspices of the American Institute of Physics, New York, ISBN 0-88318-491-5)

10. Hawking's fellow cosmologist, mathematician Roger Penrose, wrote a much more interesting book at about the same time: See Roger Penrose, *The Emperor's New Mind* (1989; reprinted 1990: Oxford University Press, Oxford, UK, New York, USA and elsewhere; ISBN 0-19-851973-7; paperback edition, Oxford University Press USA, New York, NY 10016; ISBN 978-0192861986). Penrose, interested in the nature of intelligence and our capacity to use mathematics to understand the real world, argues that the human brain is easily the most complex and interesting object in the known universe. His sense of wonder and openness to reality contrasts sharply with Hawking's world-view.

11. Fred Hoyle, *On Stonehenge* (1978: W. H. Freeman & Co., New York & London; ISBN 0716703637).

12. See Richard Dawkins, *The God Delusion* (2008: Mariner Books, Div. Houghton Mifflin Harcourt Publishers, New York, ISBN 0-618918249); Richard Dawkins, *The Blind Watchmaker* (1996: W. W. Norton & Co., New York, ISBN 0-393315703); R. Dawkins, *Climbing Mount Improbable* (1997: W. W. Norton & Co., New York, ISBN 0-393316827); and a spate of similar books *ad nauseam*. A brilliant refutation of *The God Delusion* has been written by molecular biophysicist and theologian Alistair McGrath and his wife Joanna McGrath, a neuropsychologist and theologian: See Alistair McGrath and Joanna Collicutt McGrath, *The Dawkins Delusion?* (2007:

InterVarsity Press, Downers Grove, IL 60515, ISBN 978-0-8308-3446-4).

13. Richard C. Lewontin is Agassiz Professor of Zoology and Professor of Biology at Harvard University. He is the author or co-author of several books on genetics and evolutionary change: See for example Richard C. Lewontin, *The Genetic Basis of Evolutionary Change* (1974: Columbia University Press, New York, ISBN 0-23103392-3). More recently, he has been a regular reviewer of books on evolutionary biology and related topics for the New York Review of Books, and his reviews show some tendency to claim as Dawkins does that evolution is inconsistent with belief in God.

14. See the citations in Ref. 2 to works by Ronald Numbers and Peter J. Bowler.

15. See for example Norman L. Geisler, J. Kerby Anderson, and Walter L. Bradley, *Origin Science: A Proposal for the Creation-Evolution Controversy* (1987:Baker Book House, Grand Rapids, MI 49546, ISBN 0-801038081).

CHAPTER 5: A BRIEF HISTORY OF THE INTELLIGENT DESIGN MOVEMENT

1. I can illustrate this from personal experience. Sometime during my last decade as a Professor of Theoretical Chemistry at the University of Alberta, I wrote a letter to the city newspaper criticizing an extremely dogmatic article titled *"evolution is a fact."* My letter, stating name and faculty position, questioned the use of the term "fact" in the context, pointing out that many persons with less education or fewer academic credentials than myself or the journalist writing the article would be entirely justified in rejecting such extravagant and unwarranted claims on the subject—particularly because such claims are often issued as authoritative in high school and university classrooms. A few days after my letter appeared in print I received a scathing two-page letter from a colleague in the life sciences, with copies forwarded to my Department Chairman, the Dean of the Science Faculty, and the Academic Vice-President. The writer, obviously very upset, suggested that I was not only a "fundamentalist" and a "young-earth creationist" but likely also believed in a flat earth and other superstitions. I am still surprised that a colleague should pour such abuse on another whose credentials and standing as a scientist were open to public inquiry. It is perhaps a mark of the decline in universities today that the Department Chairman merely said he thought each of us "should stick to our fields of specialization." Whatever became of "Renaissance man"?

2. See for example Peter J. Bowler, *Evolution: The History of an Idea* (1984: University of California Press, Berkeley and Los Angeles, California, ISBN 0-520-04880-6, paperback ISBN 0-520-04890-3). Bowler puts Paley's natural theology squarely in the limited context of early ideas about biology, showing how widespread philosophical controversy then existed about how to approach or understand biology. Particularly valuable is the attention given by Bowler to the historical tradition of biological classification of living things as a predecessor of evolutionary ideas. It is partly for this

reason that I have *not* treated Paley as an ID proponent.

3. Ernan McMullin, "Indifference Principle and Anthropic Principle in Cosmology". Studies in History and Philosophy of Science A, **24**, 359-389 (1993).

4. *Cf.* internet links to Discovery Institute, Seattle, WA: http://www.discovery.org; http://www.darwinsheretic.com; www.youtube.com/user/AlfredRWallaceID . Also *cf.* http://en.wikipedia.org/wiki/Alfred_Russel_Wallace; http://people.wku.edu/Charles.Smith/Wallace/BIOG.htm for very different views of Wallace. These latter show that presenting Wallace as an early advocate of intelligent design is at best problematic, given his later interest in spiritualism and other strange things.

5. Charles B. Thaxton, Walter L. Bradley and Roger L. Olsen, *The Mystery of Life's Origin: Reassessing Current Theories.* (1984: Philosophical Library, Inc., New York. ISBN 8022-2447-4). A short time before publication of this book I participated with Charles Thaxton and another scientist in a short course offered at Regent College on origins issues and first became acquainted with arguments he was making about "chemical evolution."

6. Michael Denton, *Evolution: A Theory in Crisis* (1986: Adler and Adler Publishing, Inc., Chevy Chase, MD USA 20815; ISBN 978-0917561054).

7. Michael Pitman, *Adam and Evolution* (1984: Rider and Co., London, ISBN 978-0091553906; reprinted in paperback 1987, Baker Book House Company, Grand Rapids, MI, USA 49516, ISBN 0-8010-7101-1).

8. Phillip E. Johnson, *Darwin on Trial* (1991: Inter-Varsity Press, Downers Grove, IL 60515, ISBN 0-8308-1758-1; copyright, Regnery Gateway Inc., Washington, DC 20036).

9. William A. Dembski, *Intelligent Design: The Bridge Between Science and Theology* (1991: Inter-Varsity Press, Downers Grove, IL 60515, ISBN 0-8308-1581-3). See also William A. Dembski, *The Design Inference: Eliminating Chance through Small Probabilities* (1998: Cambridge University Press, Cambridge, UK; paperback ed., 2006, Cambridge Univ. Press, ISBN 978-0521678674).

10. William A. Dembski and Jonathan Wells, *The Design of Life: Signs of Intelligence in Biological Systems* (2008, The Foundation for Thought and Ethics, Dallas, TX 75428; ISBN 978-0-9800213-0-1)

11. Walter R. Thorson, *Fingerprinting God? Divine Agency and 'Intelligent Design'.* CRUX, Vol. 39, *pp.* 2-10 (2000).

12. Stephen C. Meyer, *Signature in the Cell: DNA and the Evidence for Intelligent Design.* (2010: paperback edition, HarperCollins Publishers, New York, NY 10022, ISBN 978-0-06-14279-4).

13. See Walter R. Thorson, *Naturalism and Design in Biology: Is* Intelligent Dialogue *Possible?* and references cited there: Perspectives on Science and Christian Faith [PSCF: Journal of the American Scientific Affiliation], Vol. 56, *pp.* 26-35 (2004).

14. Michael J. Behe, *Darwin's Black Box: The Biochemical Challenge to Evolution*

(1996: The Free Press, division of Simon & Schuster, Inc., New York, ISBN 0-684-82754-9).

15. Behe's publications related to intelligent design are listed with his other scientific publications on his webpage as a member of the Lehigh Biological Sciences Department Faculty.

16. Michael J. Behe, *The Edge of Evolution: The Search for the Limits of Darwinism*. (2007: The Free Press, division of Simon & Schuster, Inc., New York, ISBN 978-0-7432-9620-5).

17. Del Ratzsch, "*Design: What Scientific Difference Could It Make?*", PSCF: JASA Vol. 56, *pp.26-37*, 2004).

18. This includes the book about "junk DNA" by Jonathan Wells: "*The Myth of Junk DNA*" (2011: Center for Science and Culture, a program of the Discovery Institute, Seattle, WA 98104, ISBN 978-1-9365990-0-4). Although (unlike Wells) I am *not* a biologist or biochemist by training, I pointed out in articles published in March 2000 that segments of DNA called *introns* (or "junk DNA") were even then beginning to be understood as having a role affecting biological function in important ways. Wells' book develops the subject much more fully; but there is nothing in his scientific discussion that depends uniquely on the ID hypothesis as a platform for scientific investigation.

GREGORY W. CARMER RESPONSE

19. Fourth Day Things, pg 11.

20. Dennett, Daniel. *Darwin's Dangerous Idea* (New York, NY: Simon and Schuster, 1996) p. 21 sited, Miller, Keith, *Finding Darwin's God*, (New York, NY: Harper, 2007) p12-13.

21. Krulwich, Robert, interview with Richard Dawkins, "In Defense of Darwin?" 92nd St. YMCA, New York City, NY, Jul 13, 2009 (http://www.radiolab.org/blogs/radiolab-blog/2009/jul/13/in-defense-of-darwin/), accessed November 3, 2012

22. Krulwich.

23. Cf. Dembski, "We need to realize that methodological naturalism is the functional equivalent of a full-blown philosophical naturalism." *Intelligent Design*, (Downers Grove: InterVarsity Press, 1999) p. 119.

24. Behe defines irreducible complexity as "a single system composed of several well-matched, interacting parts that contribute to the basic function, wherein the removal of any one of the parts causes the system to effectively cease functioning." To this definition he adds that an "irreducibly complex system cannot be produced directly by slight, successive modifications of a precursor system." *Darwin's Black Box* (New York, NY: The Free Press, 1996) p. 39.

25. Dembski argues that when we find contingency, complexity and specification there we have the marks of design which points towards intelligence. *Intelligent Design* p. 128.

26. Augros, Robert & George Stanciu. *The New Biology: Discovering the Wisdom in Nature*. (Boston: New Science Library, 1987) p 158f

27. ibid. p. 160.

28. Eldredge, Niles and S. J. Gould. "Punctuated equilibria: An alternative to phyletic gradualism" in T.J.M. Schopf, ed., *Models in Paleobiology*. San Francisco: Freeman Cooper, 1972 pp. 82-115. Reprinted in N. Eldredge *Time frames*. Princeton: Princeton Univ. Press, 1985, pp. 193-223.

CHAPTER 6: BIOLOGICAL COMPLEXITY AND BIOLOGICAL FUNCTION

1. An interesting case revealing different professional biases in scientific sub-communities occurred in the controversy over "cold fusion" in the 1990's. At the time, I was a faculty member in the University of Alberta Chemistry Department, of which electrochemist Stanley Pons had at one time been a member. (Pons and his colleague in electrochemistry Martin Fleischmann were at the University of Utah when the "cold fusion" papers appeared). For a review of the cold fusion controversy, see (for example) the following internet websites: http://en.wikipedia.org/wiki/Cold_fusion;http://undsci.berkeley.edu/article/0_0_0/cold_fusion_04; http://www.nndb.com/people/449/000044317. It is now widely agreed that cold fusion is an instance of inadequate research, though a very small minority still claim there may be a minute effect. At the time, however, the matter was debated intensely at Alberta. Those in the university faculty who were *chemists* tended to accept the results as possibly legitimate, while those who thought more like *physicists* tended to be radically dismissive of the claims made.

2. See Michael Polanyi's discussion of the role of personal judgment in making objective decisions based on probability theory: *cf.* Part One, Chapter 2, Michael Polanyi, *Personal Knowledge: Towards a Post-Critical Philosophy* (1958: Routledge and Kegan Paul, London, UK; paperback edition, 1974: University of Chicago Press, Chicago, IL, USA; and many subsequent reprintings by other publishers, including Harper & Row, 1977). Current paperback editions,, ISBN-10:0226672883; ISBN-13:978-0226672885).

3. This positive evidence for the sufficiency of "chance" is provided in equilibrium statistical thermodynamics, in which the thermodynamic properties of mechanical systems are derived by treating detailed molecular dynamics as random, and asserting that the most probable distribution of dynamical properties in a statistical ensemble is sufficient to predict thermodynamic laws. The validity of such claims for systems far from equilibrium is less clear. It's obvious, then, that attributing biological innovation to "random mutations" needs further explanation.

4. If arguments for ID were presented as natural theology, they would certainly be legitimate, though they might not necessarily be *true*.

5. Harry Cook and Hank D. Bestman, "Biological Complexity", PSCF 63, No.

3, *pp*. 159-169 (September 2011).

6. Randy Isaac, "Information, Intelligence and the Origins of Life", PSCF 63, No. 4, *pp*. 219-230 (December 2011).

7. Jonathan K. Watts, "Biological Information, Molecular Structure, and the Origins Debate", PSCF 63, No. 4, *pp*.231-239 (December 2011).

8. William A. Dembski, *Intelligent Design: The Bridge Between Science and Theology*, Part II, Section 6.5, *pp. 170-171*. (1999: InterVarsity Press, P.O. Box 1400, Downers Grove, IL, USA 60515; ISBN 0-8308-1581-3)

9. Stephen J. Freeland, "The Evolutionary Origins of Genetic Information," PSCF 63, No. 4, *pp*. 240-254 (December 2011).

10. Freeland defines "Category 1" as the set of (scientific?) propositions that have been falsified, and "Category 2", the set of (scientific?) propositions not yet falsified. This (somewhat old-fashioned) classification reflects the tradition of analytic philosophy and the ideas of Karl Popper in particular [See Karl R. Popper, *Objective Knowledge: An Evolutionary Approach* (1972: Oxford University Press, Oxford, UK; reprinted with corrections 1973; paperback edition, OUP, ISBN 0-19-875024-2)].

11. See endnote 49 in S. J. Freeland's article for a citation to a recent Cairns-Smith book developing that author's arguments about clay substrates as a possible framework for prebiotic evolution. However, an earlier criticism of Cairns-Smith's ideas remains true today: The complex structures in clays he proposes as substrates are fundamentally an *ordering* arising from minute thermodynamic and energetic considerations; these should properly be distinguished (as many ID proponents argue, esp. W. A. Dembski) from "CSI" (complex specified information); CSI (unlike the ordered patterns discussed by Cairns-Smith) cannot be reduced to a much smaller equivalent syntactical content. There is a definite limit on the physical range over which Cairns-Smith-type ordering is propagated, and energetic considerations ultimately dictate it. In DNA or RNA, on the other hand, while stereochemical forces control short-range ordering, there is no evidence for a truly long-range physical interaction that might either statically or dynamically account for CSI in some plausible way. Speculations in the 1950's and 1960's about such possibilities have never been supported by physical evidence.

12. Of course, Behe uses the bacterial flagellum as an example of *irreducible complexity* requiring "intelligent design" to explain it. My aim here is simply to illustrate the fact of its complexity—not to agree with Behe's argument.

13. T. Minamino and K. Namba, "Self-Assembly and Type III Protein Export of the Bacterial Flagellum". Journal of Molecular Microbiology and Biotechnology, **7**, pp. 5-17 (2004). This follows up research pioneered by Robert M. Macnab; see a review by Macnab in ASM (American Society for Microbiology) News, Volume 66, pp. 738-745 (2000); and earlier citations: R.M. Macnab, Journal of Bacteriology 181, pp. 7149-7153 (1999); L. Nguyen, I.T. Paulsen, J. Tchieu, C.J. Hueck and M.H. Saier, Jr., J. Mol. Microbiol.

Biotechnol. 2, 125-144 (2000). Finally, see especially Howard C. Berg, "Motile Behavior of Bacteria", *Physics Today* 53 (No. 1) *pp.* 24-29 (January 2000). These citations make clear that the system is described routinely in functional terms (as a machine would be) by people doing research on the *flagellum*.

14. Xiche Hu and Klaus Schulten, "How Nature Harvests Sunlight", *Physics Today* 50 (No. 8, Part 1), 28-34 (August 1997). *Physics Today* commonly presents accounts of research of broad current interest for members of the American Physical Society who are laymen (rather than professionals) in the field described. More complete citation of articles on the work in professional journals is given at the end of the article, but the above citation is more readable for those even less familiar with the physical sciences than myself.

15. *Loc. Cit.,* Ref. 2 above: Michael Polanyi, *Personal Knowledge: Towards a Post-Critical Philosophy* . In the present connection, see especially Part Four, Chapter 11, "The Logic of Achievement", Sections 2-4.

16. A similar distinction is important in thinking about those physical entities and structures that can be used as computers, and the logic of a Turing machine, which all computers embody. And surely it is also very easy there to jump to the conclusion that such an isomorphism must be the result of intelligent design!

17. Michael J. Behe, *Darwin's Black Box: The Biochemical Challenge to Evolution* (1996: The Free Press, division of Simon & Schuster, Inc., New York, ISBN 0-684-82754-9). See also Michael J. Behe, *The Edge of Evolution: The Search for the Limits of Darwinism.* (2007: The Free Press, division of Simon & Schuster, Inc., New York, ISBN 978-0-7432-9620-5).

18. Jianzhi Zhang, "Evolution by Gene Duplication: An Update" (Review, *Trends in Ecology and Evolution* 18, *pp.* 292-298 (June 2003)).

19. Denis O. Lamoureux, "Darwinian Theological Insights: Toward an Intellectually Fulfilled Christian Theism. Part I: Divine Creative Action and Intelligent Design in Nature." PSCF 64, No. 2 , *pp.* 108-119 (June 2012).

20. Michael B. Foster, *Mystery and Philosophy* (originally published 1957: SCM Press Ltd., London, UK, in series *The Library of philosophy and theology,* ISBN 0-31320792-5; *out of print.* Reprinted 1980, with permission of SCM Press Ltd., by Greenwood Press, a div. of Congressional Information Service, Inc., 88 Post Road West, Westport, Connecticut, USA 06881). Foster's book offers powerful insight into modern cultural decline.

21. Austin Farrer, *Faith and Speculation: An Essay in Philosophical Theology.* (original edition 1967: A. & C. Black, Ltd., London, UK. Paperback edition, 1988: printed by Page Bros., LTD., Norwich, UK, for T. & T. Clark Ltd., 59 George Street, Edinburgh, UK EH2 2LQ).

RANDY ISAAC RESPONSE

22. In his work The *Phenomenon of Man,* Harper & Row, 1961, Teilhard de

Chardin portrays the cosmos as evolving from matter to humanity to a reunion with Christ. He used the term "Omega Point" to refer to the end goal of evolution, the maximum level of complexity and consciousness. In this sense, Christ emerges from the process of evolution.

23. Stuart A Kauffman, *Reinventing the Sacred: A New View of Science, Reason, and Religion,* Basic Books, 2008. Kauffman describes how complex entities emerge through collective interaction of constituent parts. The degree to which this occurs is so astounding that he refers to this emergence as a sacred characteristic of the material world.

24. This statement does not preclude any spiritual or psychological function. It merely observes from a physical perspective, reproduction is the single event without which a lineage ceases to exist. Many physical, psychological, and spiritual functions can influence that self-replication.

DAVID LAHTI RESPONSE

25. By "indirectly" I mean that in some cases natural selection organizes a system that itself is able to respond adaptively or proactively in certain situations. The human mind/brain is like this; many of the things we can do with it are not themselves products of natural selection, but are products of such products, so to speak. We cannot say that natural selection is directly responsible for my speaking a language that people around me can understand, for instance. But natural selection can be invoked in the evolution of linguistic and underlying cognitive faculties such as learning that made this development possible.

26. Randy Isaac's fourth and weakest sense of teleology; see his contribution, above.

CHAPTER 7: THE WOODPECKER'S PURPOSE

1. This famous remark (or a variation on it) has been attributed to the evolutionary biologist G. G. Simpson.

2. Walter M. Elsasser, *The Chief Abstractions of Biology* (1975: North-Holland Publishing Co., Amsterdam, Netherlands).

3. In this connection, see Randy Isaac's comments on "emergence" as a feature of the natural order in Chapter 6.

4. Terrence W. Deacon, *Incomplete Nature: How Mind Emerged from Matter* (2012: W. W. Norton and Co., New York, NY, USA; London, UK; hardback ed., ISBN 978-0-393-04991-6).

5. A philosophical response to emergent evolution in relation to the Christian doctrine of creation has been given by Jacob Klapwijk. See Jacob Klapwijk, *Purpose in the Living World? Creation and Emergent Evolution.* (2008: English edition translated and edited by Harry Cook. Cambridge University Press, New York, NY USA; hardcover edition, ISBN 978-0-521-49340-6; paperback, ISBN 978-0-521-72943-7)

Klapwijk's book discusses many issues that also concern us here.

6. Lesslie Newbigin, *Christianity in a Pluralistic Society.* (paperback ed. 1989, Wm B. Eerdmans Publ. Co., Grand Rapids, MI, USA; ISBN 978-0-802-80426-6).

7. My point is reinforced by a "reflexive" comment: Deacon (for example) argues that his account of the emergence of human social behavior is *true*. There is no use in making such an argument if in fact human social behavior is merely an artifact of evolution, and means nothing more. Were that to be the case, human social behavior *is* only what it *is*, and "truth" is quite irrelevant to the matter.

8. See John F. Haught, "*Why Do Gods Persist? A Polanyian Reflection*", Tradition and Discovery (Journal of the Polanyi Society) 28, No. 1, *pp*. 5-15 (2001-2002). Haught's critique of Dawkins and others who argue for evolutionary theory as "complete" closely parallels my comments on Deacon's arguments about "completing nature." I am indebted to Professor Craig M. Story for drawing this article to my attention.

Austin Farrer
Faith & Speculation
c. p.161

Made in the USA
Lexington, KY
04 July 2014